Contact the author:
askagen@me.com

Contact the publisher:
Unprecedented Press LLC - 495 Sleepy Hollow Ln, Holland, MI USA 49423
www.unprecedentedpress.com | info@unprecedentedpress.com
twitter: @UnprecdntdPress | instagram: unprecedentedpress

Unless otherwise indicated, all Scripture quotations are taken from the Holy Bible, New Living Translation, copyright © 1996, 2004, 2007 by Tyndale House Foundation. Used by permission of Tyndale House Publishers, Inc., Carol Stream, Illinois 60188. All rights reserved.

ISBN-13: 978-1-7321964-4-5

Ingram Printing & Distribution, 2018
Published in the United States.

Second Edition

Unprecedented
Press

Thank God It's Monday

Everyday Evangelism
for Everyday People

Arne G. Skagen

Endorsements

Corrie Ten-Boom, who had a beautiful way of simplifying complex spiritual issues, once said KEEP IT SIMPLE, SAINT- THE KISS METHOD OF THEOLOGY! Arne Skagen has captured this kind of simplicity well in his book, "Thank God It's Monday". His refreshing subtitle "Everyday Evangelism for Everday People," would have made Auntie Corrie smile.

Arne brings evangelism down from theological ivory towers and complicated philosophy to the simple task that simply challenges us to tell people about Jesus. His personal illustrations, practical tips and biblical insights give the reader an opportunity for the Word of God to inspire them to conquer some of the fears that many of us have when it comes to sharing our faith.

Thank God it's Monday has sold well in Arne's native Norway, and along with this endorsement, I have sent up some prayers that it will have an even greater success worldwide so that the normal, everyday Christian can regularly participate in everyday evangelism. The sad fact is, surveys across the evangelical world show that most Christians do not enjoy the joy of a consistent lifestyle of evangelism. Arne's book, Lord willing, will help turn that around. May God fill you with the faith that comes from hearing God's Word (Romans 10:17) to take Arne's principles and, like a wise fisherman casting his net into the right place, bring in a "catch" of redeemed sinners.

– Danny Lehmann, Leader of YWAM in Hawaii

Thank God it's Monday is a tremendously valuable resource for every member of the church. It is simple yet transformative in it's approach to sharing the gospel. It can be read repeatedly with significant impact. It is both practical and accessible. If the principles shared in this book are truly embraced then it can change your life, change your church, maybe even change the world! Thank God for Thank God it's Monday!

– *Steve Wilkins, Leader Ministries Without Borders, Canada*

Thank God It's Monday, every day evangelism for ordinary people, is one of the most useful resources I have come across for helping people move naturally in the area of personal evangelism. I have personally known the author of the book for over 15 years and have heard him teach and impart the message of this book in many forums, conferences and churches. I can attest to the amazing fruit produced in people's lives and the impact on many church's because of the simple unchanging truths that Arne has communicated. He has an unique ability to equip and empower people toward effective harvesting. His life, gift and the message contained in this book has had a significant impact on my life personally and on my family. It has empowered the churches, discipleship programs and leadership schools that I have responsibility for, and I have found that it has provoked a fresh, expectant harvest mindset in us all. I strongly recommend this book for individuals and churches who desire to get the tools to JUST DO IT in the area of spirit-led everyday evangelism.

– *Andrew Hughes, Leader of the Point Church Network*

I'm thrilled that this book is now available in English, after the runaway success of the original Norwegian edition. I have worked with my friend Arne Skagen for many years: reading 'Thank God it's Monday' is just like listening to Arne in person. His unique ability to equip the church to reach everyday people in everyday evangelism is not a theory; it's Arne's lifestyle. In this essential book Arne shares that lifestyle with us in a way that always encourages and inspires. Most important, what Arne writes really works; I have seen the tangible results time after time. If you read one book on evangelism, read this one. I highly recommend it.

– *Roger Aubrey Leader, All Nations Church, Cardiff, UK*

Thank God it's Monday by Arne Skagen of Bergen, Norway is a wonderful and compelling book that is very practical and deeply encouraging. Through his use of real life stories and principles, Arne takes his readers on a journey through the important phases of sharing the good news of Jesus Christ. As Arne writes about the importance of loving people, listening to the voice of the Holy Spirit, and hearing "the Harvest Language," he shows himself to be an evangelist who knows how to equip his readers with the ability to share their faith with confidence and great boldness. I highly recommend this very helpful and insightful book.

– *Bill Clark, Church Leader at New Life Church, Ministries Without Borders Canada*

Contents

Preface

My life has been an amazing journey since the day I decided to give my life to Jesus Christ and follow Him. The journey has been filled with exciting adventures and challenges with both victory and defeat. I am so grateful to the Lord who called me, and who has placed me in an abundant harvest working alongside my fellow brothers and sisters all around the world.

I wish to dedicate this book to my wife Kjersti, my best friend and co-laborer in ministry; and to Silje, Sunniva, Solvor and Svanhild; my four amazing daughters, who have had to share their dad with so many others for many years.

I would also like to thank my close friends and colleagues in Kristent Nettverk and in Ministries without Borders, who I have closely worked alongside for the past twelve years. You have challenged and inspired me in the ministry of the Kingdom of God.

A special thanks to Erlend Evenstand, who with his gifted editing skills has been invaluable in the manuscript process.

Finally, I would like to thank all of those working in the harvest who faithfully follow the Lord of the Harvest day after day to reach those who have yet to accept Him. Be encouraged! The Great Commission will be accomplished, because Jesus is "with you always, even unto the end of the world ."

Introduction

You wake up in bed, rested and ready for a new week. Thank God it's Monday! Full of expectation for the day that has just begun, you go to the bathroom, look in the mirror and think "I am loved" and start talking with the One who loves you.

Evangelism begins every Monday morning in the bathroom. It springs from an intimate and living relationship between you and God. He fills you with his love, joy and peace so that his life can overflow and touch your friends, neighbours, colleagues and all of those who you'd love to know the love of Jesus. It's about reaching out with God's power and love in a relaxed and natural way. It's about reaching your social network – where God has placed you with a purpose.

Thank God It's Monday is not for you if you're looking for techniques or methods of evangelism. This book does not describe a human method, but a heavenly strategy where we take a walk with the Holy Spirit through our neighbourhood, in our circle of friends and at our workplace – wherever people hang out and live. It's about seeing what the Holy Spirit sees, hearing what he hears and being obedient when he tells us to act. This is the lifestyle I want to share with you – and the reason I wrote this book.

You are surrounded by a ripe harvest, and so is your church community. We have seen this happen in many places over quite a long period of time – not just once, but time and time again – of how God has transformed an inward-looking church community into a vibrant and active body. Seeing people get saved every day is not an unrealistic goal. The Lord of the Harvest wants to teach us how to see the harvest and how to gather it in.

The harvest is plentiful, and the harvest is ripe. Jesus is right about that. As you read this book, my prayer is that the Holy Spirit will speak to you and give you faith to see things happen; that evangelism will no longer just be something you have to do – or something you do with a guilty conscience. Instead it will flow naturally from our lives – with the Holy Spirit's help. We'll wake up on Monday mornings with great expectations of what "God in us" can do.

Does this sound at all like a *method*? It is quite the opposite; it is a *heavenly strategy*.

May the grace of Jesus Christ, the love of God and the Holy Spirit be with you all as you bring in the harvest.

Arne Skagen
Bergen, Norway,
November 2013

Comments

The names of the people mentioned in the stories and examples throughout this book have been altered to protect their privacy. I wanted this book to give examples and stories from real life events, which is why I have chosen to use real stories from everyday life. I was not able to gain permission to share these stories from everyone involved, and have therefore chosen to make the people in these stories anonymous.

1

Driven By Love

God's Love at a Retirement Home

Sara works at a retirement home. She loves these elderly people, and has prayed often for them. One day her love drives her into action: She goes to her boss and asks if she could invite som friends from church to come and talk and pray with the residents.

The director seems a bit surprised, but after giving it some thought he tells her that yes, she'd be allowed to do this but on one condition: "As long as it is done in a respectful manner.

I am a friend of Sara's, and one of the two friends she invited from church to come along with her to the retirement home one afternoon.

It is interesting to meet these people who have lived a long life. Many of them have a lot to talk about. As the conversations get more personal, it becomes evident that many of them feel a bit uneasy about the future. They've reached the age of their life expectancy. For all intents and purposes the retirement home could be their last stop in life. What happens afterwards? Is there anything more to hope for?

We chat with the elderly people and share the Gospel with them. We tell them about God's plan of salvation, about why Jesus came and about what he can give: a future and hope. Some of them start to tear up a bit. Others take hold of our hands and tell us that they are so happy that we are here.

Seated at one of the tables is a lady named Judith. She's been listening intently while we shared the Gospel. When we ask her what she thinks about what we shared, she answers:

"I believe."

We sit down with her at a table, take out the Bible and read this verse:

"If you confess with your mouth that Jesus is Lord and believe in your heart that God raised him from the dead, you will be saved."[1]

---

1   Romans 10:9

"Do you want to receive Jesus Christ as your Lord and Saviour?" we ask her. With a loud and clear voice Judith sincerely answers, "Yes, I do." And, in a few simple words, she invites Jesus into her heart. Judith is the first one to get saved that day, but not the last one: During the course of the afternoon five more people make a decision to follow Christ.

With Sara leading the way, the residents begin to have prayer meetings, read the Bible, drink coffee and socialize. This is happening a few times a week, at a nothing-out-of-the-ordinary retirement home.

The Driving Force is God's Love

It is not a coincidence that my first example is the story of Sara, because she shows us what needs to be the driving force of all evangelism, God's love.

God loves people. God loves all people with a love that was willing to sacrifice everything. "For God loved the world so much that he gave his one and only Son, so that everyone who believes in him will not perish but have eternal life."[2]

Evangelism is not about us or what we can achieve. It is about God and what he can do through his son Jesus.

The Bible continues by telling us: "For we know how dearly God

---

2   John 3:16

loves us, because he has given us the Holy Spirit to fill our hearts with his love."[3] It is this love that is the driving force when we share Jesus with other people. "Christ's love compels us."[4]

I have met many Christians that have a guilty conscience when it comes to evangelism. They know that they *should* share the Gospel with others, but they find evangelism to be an unpleasant duty and a heavy burden. "Well, if that's the way you feel about it, don't even *think* about sharing the Gospel!" This answer surprises a lot of people. Some even feel provoked: "Don't you *want* people to hear the Gospel? Don't you *care* about people getting saved?"

Of course I do! But the Gospel is the *good news*; it is the message of God's love to us through Jesus Christ. That is why it is so important that the delivery of the message matches its content, that the messenger does not contradict the message. If we are driven by duty or by a guilty conscience, or both, we will have a hard time conveying God's love and we might as well not do it.

> *The Gospel is about God's love. What drives Sara is not a sense of duty or a guilty conscience, but God's love.*

The Good News is about God's love. Sarah isn't motivated by a sense of duty or a bad conscience, but only by God's love. The love God has for the people at the retirement home has

---

3   Romans 5: 5
4   2 Corinthians 5:14

infected Sara. That is why she is not only *sharing* the Good News, but goes around the retirement home *being* the Good News to people.

God's Love at a Coffee Shop

One day I was sitting at a coffee shop with a church leader discussing important things about the Kingdom of God over a cup of coffee. After we had been talking for awhile, a woman with two small children sat down at the table next to us.

As we continued to talk, I got an impression of God's love for this woman and her two children. I didn't see any writing on the wall, nor did I hear a voice from above. I just quietly felt God's love for a mother and her two children.

We continued to talk. Now and then the impression resurfaced and I found myself thinking about the three people at the next table. I thought about them, but that was all I did with the thought. I didn't want to end the conversation with the church leader. After all, we were discussing important things that had to do with the Kingdom of God.

Finally, the woman got up from her table and left the coffee shop with her two children. As the door closed behind her, I turned to the church leader and asked: "Do you know that woman?" He shook his head and said: "I don't really know her, but I do know her name."

That night I continued to think about the woman and her children. I wasn't able to put the experience in the coffee shop behind me. I finally decided to get online and look up her phone number. I wasn't feeling particularly confident as I dialled the number.

"Good evening. My name is Arne Skagen," I said. "I'm not sure if you remember me, but I sat next to your table at the coffee shop earlier today. I was having a conversation with another man." The phone went quiet for a few moments. Then she answered: "Thinking about it, yes, I do remember two men sitting at the table next to us." Hesitantly I decided to tell her why I was calling. "When I saw you and your two children at the coffee shop today, God reminded me of something, and that is why I am calling you. I believe God wants you to know that he sees you. He loves you, and he has good plans for you and your children."

When we finished the conversation a few minutes later, the woman told me that she was grateful for what I had shared with her. She thanked me for calling.

A few days later I received an email from my friend telling me that the woman had showed up at a meeting the following Sunday. After the meeting the woman had let them know that she wanted to receive Jesus.

Live Close to Jesus

I will be telling lots of stories in this book. In many of these stories I play a part. However, I only play a small part.

The main character is the Holy Spirit. He is always the one who plays the main part when Jesus becomes real to people. Because the Holy Spirit lives within us, he invites us to work alongside him, and we get to play an important part in what he is doing.

What am I trying to convey through the two stories I just shared with you? They show us the most common way the Holy Spirit leads us: His love "speaks" to us and moves us toward other people.

But in order for this to happen, we have to live close to Jesus.

> *The more intimate our relationship with Jesus is, the more we are drawn close to those he loves.*

We can see in the Gospels how important fellowship with the Father was to Jesus. He prioritized this above all else. Even on busy days when the people made a lot of demands on him, he found time to be alone with his Father. He often went up to a mountain. In the Bible the mountain represents the place where revelation is given. It is on a mountain that God reveals his face; it is where he exposes his inner being.

Moses experienced the same thing. While the Israelites were occupied with how God could meet their needs, Moses, who was the leader of the people, focused on something entirely different. He was occupied with God himself. Moses was called up to the mountain to meet with God. It was on the mountain where he became acquainted with God, and God counted him as his friend.

King David was called a man after God's own heart.[5] He was in no way blameless, but he was a man who trusted in God. He experienced in many situations that "The Lord is a friend to those who fear him. He teaches them his covenant."[6]

God wants the same thing for us: that we may know him, so that he can share things with us in confidence. "I pray for you constantly, asking God, the glorious Father our Lord Jesus Christ, to give you spiritual wisdom and insight so that you might grow in your knowledge of God."[7]

Evangelism is not an activity but a natural expression of our relationship with Jesus.

When we know God, live close to Jesus and are filled with the Holy Spirit, we can meet people in a safe and trusting way. We know our Father who knows all people. When we carry his presence within us, the people we meet will experience Gods' love.

Resting and Trusting in the Holy Spirit

When you have an opportunity to share the Gospel with someone, you can quickly be gripped by fear – more accurately,

---

5 1 Samuel 13:14
6 Psalms 25:14
7 Ephesians 1:7

a "fear of man". Anxious thoughts might build up in your mind: "What will he think of me if I say this? Will he ignore me, laugh at me or speak badly of me? What if I can't find the right words? What if he doesn't understand a thing of what I'm trying to explain?"

You are not the only one with these thoughts. Many of us have experienced this. Welcome to the club.

Let us look closer at the fear of man. Notice what happens when the fear of man affects you: All of a sudden everything becomes about "I, me and mine". Suddenly I am in the front and God is shoved into the background. All the attention is focused on *my* thoughts, *my* emotions, and *my* fears. My thoughts end up becoming defensive and negative.

I can choose, at least to a great degree, what I do with the fear of man: Will it control me, or will I control it? Here is some advice:

> *Focus on what Jesus thinks about the person you are talking to, rather than on what the person you are talking to is thinking about you.*

When I do this, I often experience the truth that "Perfect love drives out all fear." As long as we are driven by a sincere desire for people to experience God's love, my experience is that many people usually have a positive response.

God has chosen to use ordinary people like you and me to share the Gospel. Paul writes: "We now have this light shining in our hearts, but we ourselves are like fragile clay jars containing great treasure". Why? "... this makes it clear that our great power is from God, not from ourselves."[8] That is why we don't get blinded by our own weaknesses and failures. We remain focused on the great treasure: the exciting reality that the Kingdom of God is near.

The Kingdom of God is so near that the Holy Spirit lives within us. That is why I now and then have to remind myself: "Arne – *chin up*! Lift up your gaze! Remember that the Holy Spirit lives inside of you." The fact that the Holy Spirit lives in us makes an enormous difference (I will discuss this more in Chapters 3 and 4). With him we can meet new people and situations from a place of rest as we trust in him.

A few years back I was visiting some friends in the United States. They belonged to a church in Illinois that had a heart for the city they lived in. Every Saturday some of the church members would go and visit one of the state prisons there. They brought food and drinks for the prisoners, and then would sing and preach the Gospel. When my friends asked me if I wanted to come along, I said yes. In the car on the way to the prison, one of my friends turned to me and said: "I forgot to tell you something: Today *you* are the one who is going to preach the Gospel!" At first I thought that they weren't serious, like it was some friendly practical joke. But no one in the car was

---

8   2 Corinthians 4:7

laughing, and soon I realized that they were serious.

That's when I felt fear grab hold of me. "I'll soon be face to face with some of the most hardened criminals in Illinois! What on earth can I say to convince them?" Negative thoughts and experiences began to line up in my head; in only a few seconds these thoughts had handcuffed all of my boldness.

We arrived at the prison and were taken into a room where prisoners – about 30 – had already arrived along with several guards.

Frantic thoughts filled my head: "Jesus, I can't do this! I have no idea what to say!"

While my friends (if I could still call them friends, at that moment I wasn't so sure) started to sing and play, I tried to gather my thoughts. I told myself: "Arne, Jesus has called you to follow him. He has called you to share the Good News. He has promised to be with you all the days of your life, including today. Share what is on your heart, and God will make sure that what you share will touch *their* hearts."

I would be lying if I told you that I stood in front of those prisoners without being nervous or without the fear of man. With my knees feeling that they were about to buckle under me, I stood up and shared in a few simple sentences what God had done for me and how he has filled my life with love.

I also told them that Jesus came to set prisoners free. When I was done, I took a deep breath and looked out on the assembly: "Jesus is here right now. He can set you free. He wants to free you from your past and give you a new future."

I could not believe my own eyes when some of the prisoners stood up and came forward. One by one they came to the front, until over half of them had given their lives to Jesus – along with a few of the guards!

That Saturday I realized that, even though I may feel the fear of man or feel that I am inadequate, I must never forget who lives within me, and who is with me all the days of my life.

I have to mention that I am still friends with the people in the church in Illinois. Today I can even be grateful to them for giving me that "opportunity" to grow and to learn!

Carried by Prayer

I don't want to finish off the first chapter until I've mentioned something about prayer. It is vital that evangelism is powered by God's love. But it is equally important that it is *powered by prayer*.

All evangelism starts with prayer. John Wesley emphasized this when he said "All of God's work is done through prayer."

Paul writes in his first letter to Timothy, "I urge you, first of all, to pray for all people. Ask God to help them; intercede on their behalf, and give thanks for them."[9] In the same passage he explains why prayer is so important. God "wants everyone to be saved and [to] understand the truth."[10]

As we pray, we are clearing the way for God, just like John the Baptist cleared the way for Jesus. "Prepare the way for the Lord's coming! Clear the road for him! The valleys will be filled, and the mountains and hills made level. The curves will be straightened, and the rough places made smooth. And then all people will see the salvation sent from God."[11]

In the lives of the people that we pray for, there are high mountains and deep valleys, crooked roads and rocky paths that prevent them from receiving God's salvation. "Prepare the way for the Lord's coming!" is a call to all those who pray, and it is a strategy that can be used in the work of prayer.

But *how* should we pray? It is not always easy to know how to pray. "...we do not know what we should pray about in order to pray accurately." Fortunately we have the Holy Spirit, for "the Holy Spirit prays for us with groaning that cannot be expressed in words."[12] He knows the people we're praying for. He knows about the high mountains and the deep valleys in their lives; he knows where the road is crooked and where the rough places are.

---

9   1 Timothy 2:1
10 1 Timothy 2:4
11 Luke 3:4-6
12 Romans 8:26

The Holy Spirit knows the hindrances. That is why we do not need to spend time in prayer informing him about what he should be doing. Instead, we let the Holy Spirit *inform us*. We might even discover that we sometimes become the answer to our own prayers. When you pray for your neighbours, work colleagues or classmates, you have to be prepared for God to point the finger back at you and say: "I will bless these people through you."

This is why we have to add at the end of all of our prayers for others: *"Lord, here I am, send me"*.

Perseverance in Prayer

In the Bible there are many promises concerning prayer. "Pray, and you shall receive."[13]

"Ask me for anything in my name, and I will do it!"[14]

"If two of you agree here on earth concerning anything you ask, my Father in heaven will do it for you."[15]

Ignited by these promises, I have more than once decided to persevere in prayer for those I want to see saved. Initially it seems to work well; I pray until my knuckles are white. But after awhile my commitment begins to fade. My prayers

---

13 Matthew 7:7
14 John 14:14
15 Matthew 18:19

become fewer and I start to lose focus.

Am I the only one who has felt like this? Or have you felt like this too? Good. Then there are two of us.

Here is some advice that helped me.

Relax. Too much strained effort can suffocate your prayer life. The Lord tells those who feel burned out in prayer: "Be still, and know that I am God!"[16] Prayer is about letting the Spirit of God pray through us. It is our responsibility to be open, to listen and to be available to the Spirit.

Take notes. Find a notebook and write down the names of those you're praying for. You can also write down other things that the Holy Spirit reminds you of during your time of prayer. When the answers start coming, your notebook can be turned into a book of thanksgiving.

Find someone to partner with in prayer. Many of the promises in the Bible concerning prayer are given to two or more who are praying: "What two or more agree on here on earth ..." Find someone who shares your heart for people. Pray for each other's friends, encourage one another and keep each other accountable.

Persevere. Be motivated by Paul's word to the Galatians: "So let's not get tired of doing what is good. At just the right time

---

16 Psalm 46:10

we will reap a harvest of blessing if we do not give up."[17]

One lady that I met had prayed for her husband for 40 years. *Every single day for 40 years.* That is 14,600 days of prayer. She wasn't the only one praying; there were periods where friends from church had prayed with her.

After 40 years, something started to happen. Someone in the church contacted her husband and asked if he wanted to come to an introductory course in the Christian faith. His wife had asked him several times to come, but his answer had always been no. However, now that the question came from someone else, his answer was yes.

During the third evening of the Alpha Course, this man received Jesus into his life. Towards the end of the night he stood up and said:"For 40 years my wife has prayed for me to become a Christian. Tonight her prayers have been answered. I have decided that I want to give my life to Jesus, and I want to follow him for the rest of my life."

---

17   Galatians 6:9

2

The Harvest is Ready

A Disheartened Church

A church had invited me to do a seminar on evangelism. It was a big church with several hundred members. A large, but disheartened church. At one meeting one person after another from the church stood up and "witnessed" about how closed the city was to the Gospel, and how uninterested most people seemed.

The church had tried to reach out to new people, they really had. There was certainly no lack of initiative and programmes. From what they shared it was evident that there had been a lot of hard work, but little fruit. They had hardly seen anyone come to Christ in the last few years.

I listened to what they shared. The discouragement seemed sincere. Based on their bad experiences their discouragement was totally understandable. After awhile I decided to ask the Holy Spirit what he thought about the state of the city. Was it as hopeless as it seemed? Did he see something different than what everyone else saw? The Holy Spirit answered by filling me with expectation and excitement: An expectation for what God was going to do in that city and an excitement when thinking about the people that would experience God's love. During the meeting I shared my excitement and expectation. I then began to mention some names I believed the Holy Spirit had reminded me of (sometimes he speaks to me this way, by giving me names of people. He might speak to you differently. The Spirit can speak to us in thousands of ways.)

I called out the names.
Mary.
Martin.
Katrina.
Jerry.
Lisa.
Plus a few more – about 15 in all.

Every time I mentioned a name, I noticed that some of the people in the congregation were nodding in confirmation.

Then I said: "These people are the harvest. Let's pray for them."

When we were finished praying, I encouraged them to be bold during the next few days. "Share God's love in a way that feels natural to you." In addition I asked them to invite these people to church or to a smaller group in the church.

Many of the people answered yes to the invitations (those who had invited them thought that there were surprisingly many who had answered yes). Several of them received Jesus during the following days. Even more got saved during the weeks and months that followed.

It was all fruit that came from all of us listening to the Holy Spirit and acting on his cues.

The Harvest is Plentiful

In Luke 10 Jesus tells us that "the harvest is great".[1] He does not try to give proof for His claim. He simply states it as a fact. It is not open for discussion. The harvest *is* great. Jesus does not pray for the harvest in Luke chapter 10. Instead, he prays for the workers who are few. "Pray to the Lord who is in charge of the harvest; ask him to send more workers into his fields."

"Great harvest" means "a lot of people." That is how I have always thought of it. But I believe that Jesus is telling us something more when he uses the expression "great harvest." What *is* a harvest? A harvest denotes an advanced condition, a later phase in a process. A seed was placed in the ground. It was nourished by sunlight and water. It began to sprout and

---

1   Luke 10:2

it slowly moved through the soil, pushing towards the earth's crust. Finally, it stood tall in the field, ripe and ready to be harvested.

It's the same way with a lot of people. They have come so far in their search for God that they are like a ripe harvest. They do not need any more evidence that God exists. They don't need any more tracts, testimonies or a bowl of hot soup on the street. They need someone to notice them, take them seriously and to lead them in the last step of making a decision.

Jesus says that the harvest is great. This means that there are many people who are ready to receive him and his salvation.

You're Touching a Ripe Harvest Today

You have probably heard the expression "You can't see the wood for the trees." I tend to slightly alter it and say "You can't see the harvest for the people".

You can't see the harvest for the people.

This is the greatest challenge in harvesting: Jesus says that the harvest is great, but we do not see it.

Our greatest challenge is the enemy's most important strategy. He wants us to believe that the harvest is small, and that this small harvest will only be harvested after a lot of hard work and resistance. Our own experience often seems to confirm this: Evangelism and harvesting is hard work; with plenty of striving and with little fruit.

I believe that Jesus wants to show us ways to do the work with less striving and more fruit.

Could I share with you a dream that I had?

I was standing in the middle of a field – an enormous, vast field. It spread out as far as the eye could see. Wherever I turned, I could see a ripe harvest: plump maise, ready to be golden grain. It was an amazing sight and it filled me with excitement. But after awhile the excitement turned into frustration. I was standing in this enormous, yellow rectangle looking helplessly around. "Lord," I said, "Where should I start harvesting? Should I start over here? Or should I start at the other end and work my way from there? Where on earth should I start?"

The Lord of the harvest answered me: "*Arne, look down.*" I looked down and noticed that my feet were touching some of the ripe stalks of grain. The Lord of the harvest said: "*This is* where you are to start. You can only harvest the harvest that you are touching.

> *You can only harvest the harvest that you are touching.*

The dream filled me with joy and peace (and this confirmed that this dream came from God). When I woke up the following morning I felt relieved. I realized that I did not need to strive to find a ripe harvest. I realized that I was surrounded by it.

As you are reading this book, I'd like to encourage you to pray to the Lord of the harvest, that he may open your eyes. Let him take you on a journey. Walk with Jesus through your neighbourhood, your workplace, your friends and your family. Ask him to show you what is going on with the people in your life and what he is doing in their lives. See, hear and feel – use all of your senses. Let yourself be moved by what Jesus is showing you.

If you don't experience anything right away, don't be discouraged. You are about to venture on a journey of discovery with the Lord of the harvest. He is the teacher, and you are the student. Be patient and trust that your teacher knows what he is doing.

Jesus said to the first disciples: "Come, follow me, and I will make you fishers of men."[2] He is saying the same thing to you and me today. Some of the first things that he teaches us are that we are surrounded by a ripe harvest.

The 4M Syndrome

One day Jesus and his disciples are travelling on the road from Jerusalem to Galilee. [3] They take a shortcut through Samaria, an area many Jews chose to travel around in order to avoid

---

2   Matthew 4:19
3   John 4:1-42

meeting any of the despised Samaritans. When they arrive tired and hungry at Sychar in Samaria, the disciples go into the town to find some food. Jesus does not come along, however. Instead, he sits down at a well outside of the city. Here he meets a woman who is living a life of sin. Jesus does not condemn her; he meets her with such love that it makes her forget why she came to the well. She leaves her water jug, goes into town and says to everyone she meets, "Come and meet the man who told me everything that I have ever done!"

When the disciples find Jesus at the well, all they can think about is the fact that they're so hungry. "Rabbi, come and eat!", they say to Him. Jesus answered them by saying, "My food is to do the will of him who sent me." He then goes on to reprimand them. "You say that there are still four months till harvest. But I say: Lift your eyes and see the fields! They are ready for harvest."

A lot of Christians today have the same attitude as the disciples had in Sychar. "Not today, but things should start happening in about four month." I call it the "4M Syndrome" (Four Month Syndrome). This is quite common among God's people. We put a buffer of four months on our prayers and our expectations of God. But God says, "The right time is *now; this* is the day of salvation!"

Those four extra months represent our lack of experience (or negative experience) in harvesting. By pushing all of our expectations into the future, we shield ourselves from dis-appointment and failure today. The problem is that, at the same time, we are shielding ourselves from the opportunities that God wants to give us *here and now*. We no longer have any expectations that Jesus can save today.

The woman at the well in Sychar was not affected by the 4M Syndrome. She did not sit down to wait for a suitable time to witness about Jesus. She left her water jug and went immediately into the city. And the city was full of people ripe for the harvest. "Many of the Samaritans in the city came to believe in Jesus because of the woman's testimony." A few minutes earlier all the disciples had been in the city. They had a lot more to tell about Jesus than the Samaritan woman. But they didn't witness to anyone. The only thing they were thinking about was how they were going to get their own needs met, which in this case meant: FOOD! PRONTO! When the disciples entered the city "They could not see the harvest for the people." It was only when Jesus encouraged them to lift their eyes to see that they saw the harvest. They saw all the people who were on their way towards Jesus because of the testimony of the woman who had forgotten her own needs in her excitement to tell others about Jesus.

Today is the Day of Salvation

A young man asked me if I could pray for his mother. He told me that he had prayed many years that she would get saved. Of course I said yes. Before I started to pray, I asked the Holy Spirit, "How should I pray?" That is a question I often ask, simply because I do not know what to pray. That is why I ask the Holy Spirit who "prays for us with groaning that cannot be expressed in words." At the same time I thought, "The son is telling me that he has prayed for his mother for several years. We know that God answers prayers that are according to his will. One plus one equals two."

Sometimes we get so used to praying for someone that we don't even notice when God answers. We don't actually expect that our prayers *will* be answered. Could this be the case in this situation as well?

When I asked the Holy Spirit, I sensed that the mother did not need any more prayer. She was ready to receive Jesus, but she needed help in doing so.

"Can we call your mother?" I asked the young man. He seemed a bit surprised at first, but he got his cell phone out of his pocket and handed it to me.

"Your son has told me that he has been praying for you for several years," I told her. "That does not surprise me," his mother answered. "He is a kind and considerate boy."

"Have you ever thought about making peace with God?" I asked her. "Lately, I have actually thought quite a bit about that," she went on to say, "but I am not quite sure how to go about it." I told her how simple it was. Jesus has done everything that needs to be done in order for us to have peace with him. The only thing that we have to do is to accept his gift and give thanks. I told her what it means to receive Jesus as her Lord and Saviour, and to give her life to him.

"Would you like to do that now?" I asked her. Right away she answered yes. We prayed a simple prayer of salvation before we finished the conversation. When I handed the phone back to her son, I could see his eyes tearing up.

A church congregation was arranging an Alpha Course, and they had put an ad in the local newspaper. A man had noticed the ad and had called to find out more about the course. He was, as he told them, "a bit curious about Jesus." One of the employees at the church told him a bit about the Alpha Course, which is an introductory course to the Christian faith. Before she finished the conversation, she invited him to come to her church in two weeks when the course started. The phone conversation created excitement in the lunch room. A man had shown interest in Jesus, and was thinking about coming to the Alpha Course!

My first thought was: "How great!" My second thought was: "Two weeks? Why should the man have to wait two weeks when he's curious about Jesus today?" I asked for the man's phone number and left the lunch room. John was surprised when I called him, but he was eager to talk. He told me that he had decided to sign up for the Alpha Course at the church. While we were talking, something became clear to me. "He does not need to wait two weeks. If he wants to, he can receive Jesus today." After talking awhile on the phone, I suggested that we meet up and talk face to face. "You have time for that?" "If you like, you are welcome to come over to my house," he said. A few hours later we were sitting in his living room, me and another man from church. We continued to talk about faith in the same open and relaxed way that we had talked on the phone.

It became evident that John was more than "just a bit curious" about Jesus. When we asked him if he wanted to receive Jesus right then and there he didn't see a reason why he should postpone it. So we prayed a prayer for him. Right there on the couch in his living room, John received Jesus. Two weeks later he started the Alpha Course where he could learn more about the Jesus that he had decided to follow.

Pray "Today Prayers"!

When Jesus stood up in the synagogue in his hometown of Nazareth, he opened the scroll and read from the prophet Isaiah where it is written: "The Spirit of the Lord is upon me, for he has anointed me to bring Good News to the poor. He has sent me to proclaim that captives will be released, that the blind will see, that the oppressed will be set free, and that the time of the LORD's favour has come."[4] He then rolled up the scroll. With all eyes looking intently at him, he said: "The Scripture you've just heard has been fulfilled this very day!"
Today! Jesus himself was the fulfillment of that Scripture. He was then, and he still is today. "Jesus Christ is the same yesterday, today, and forever".[5] The most effective way to cure the "4M Syndrome" is to pray "today prayers".

---

4   Luke 4:18-19
5   Hebrews 13:8

"Lord, let me live under an open heaven – today."

"Lord, let me lift my eyes to see that the harvest is ripe – today."

"Lord, let me share the Good News with somebody – today."

"Lord, let me lead someone to you – today."

I believe these are prayers after God's own heart, since he wants "all people to be saved and to know the truth." Praying "today prayers" does something to me. It fills me with an expectation for today. It makes me exclaim "Thank God it's Monday!"

Yesterday is over, and no one knows what tomorrow will bring. But *today* I can serve the Lord, follow Jesus and be obedient to the Holy Spirit.

The Harvest is Ready

Just now, as I write the conclusion to this second chapter about the harvest being ripe, the alarm on my phone went off (No, this is not something I am saying to try to create a dramatic ending to the chapter). I almost forgot! I have an appointment to meet with Mary from the church I go to.

When we talked on the phone awhile ago, Mary told me that she felt disheartened. "I find it difficult to share the Gospel with my colleagues at work," she said. "What should I say to them? How can I reach them?" I tried to encourage her. "Mary, don't feel stressed about sharing the Gospel. God will give you opportunities that come naturally to you. Remember that when you are filled with the Holy Spirit, God's love dwells within you, and your colleagues will notice this." I challenged her to be sensitive to the leading of the Spirit in the week that lay ahead. "Perhaps someone will share some personal problems with you? That is often a signal. Why are they sharing this with you? It is because you have the answer to their challenges and problems. The answer is Jesus Christ".

A few days later, this is exactly what happened. A colleague at the retirement home where Mary works came over and confided in her. "My sickness has returned." Mary feels compassion for the woman. She remembers the conversation we had earlier: Is this a signal? She asks her colleague: "Could I pray for you together with someone from my church?" This is why my cell phone is beeping. I have to go to meet Mary, and we're going together to meet with her colleague.

Back Again

We had a nice time in the home of Mary's colleague. She lit up when we arrived at her house, and she was happy that we were there to pray for her. We laid our hands on her and asked for God's power, healing and strength into the situation. We shared the good news about Jesus with her. She wanted to receive salvation. She also wanted to be a part of the life group that Mary was a part of.

Her colleague could, of course, have found a church in her area and asked for prayer. But that would have been a longer road for her. Now, however, Jesus had been the one who had found her, through her Christian colleague. Mary had not planned to lead her colleague to Christ; she had just shown her compassion. That is often all it takes. Small actions done in great love can open up the road to faith for new people.

I was interrupted in my writing, but not derailed. That small interruption highlights what I have been trying to convey in Chapter 2: The harvest is ready! You and I see that the harvest is ripe every day. We don't have to wait four months to reap the harvest. We can do it today. *Today* is the day of salvation.

3

Sent With a Mission

The Mission Statement

At the beginning of his official ministry, Jesus went into the synagogue in Nazareth on the Sabbath just as he always had. When he stood up to read they handed him the book of Isaiah. Jesus opened the scroll to the place where it says:

"The Spirit of the Lord is on me, because he has anointed me to proclaim good news to the poor. He has sent me to proclaim freedom for the prisoners and recovery of sight for the blind, to set the oppressed free, to proclaim the year of the Lord's favor."[1]

As he closed the scroll, he said: "Today this scripture is fulfilled in your hearing."

Jesus fulfilled Isaiah's prophecy. He makes the word of the prophets his own mission statement: This is what I am here to

---

1   Luke 4:18,19

do, "to preach the good news to the poor." But Jesus was not satisfied with only preaching the good news; he demonstrated the good news in practical ways. The Gospels tell the story of how the prisoners are set free, the blind receive their sight and the oppressed are delivered.

The writer of Hebrews proclaims that "Jesus Christ is the same yesterday, today and forever." This must mean that whatever Jesus did yesterday, he will also do today. But Jesus is in heaven and is seated at the right hand of the Father. How then can he do the same things now as when he was walking on earth? Because the Church, which is his body, is now here.

To be the Church

The church is not a building with a pointy steeple. You can't stand inside the church or go to church. The church is a body. It is Jesus' body.[2] Through the church, Jesus will do the same things that he did when he lived on this earth. Through the church he will proclaim and demonstrate the reality that the kingdom of God is near. This is why the mission statement from the synagogue in Nazareth is the blueprint for how the church should work today. The blueprint tells us that we are anointed "to preach." In other words, we are anointed with a purpose.

---

2   1 Corinthians 12:27

The church is not a building made up of lifeless components. It consists of "living stones that God is building into his spiritual temple".[3] Jesus is the Cornerstone[4] in the spiritual temple, which consists of those who are filled with the Holy Spirit and who want to finish the mission that he has given us together. We as disciples do not only belong to Christ, we also belong to one another. It is when we stand together as brothers and sisters that we are able to complete the task that Jesus has given us (this point is so central to this book I've dedicated the whole last chapter to it).

The Body Begins to Function

"We are so tired of meetings and activities," the man expressed on the telephone. He said "we" because he was speaking on behalf of several people – himself, his wife and some friends. "What is it you're longing for?" I asked him. "To live the life that we read about in God's Word," he answered. "But we have no idea how to get that going."

Two weeks later we met up in their living room. There were fourteen of us. We had some sandwiches, drank some tea and shared our dreams with one another. A friend of mine taught some fundamental truths from God's Word. Afterwards we shared with each other what we believed God had given us: a personal greeting, words of encouragement and edification. We prayed for several people, and some were healed. Not everyone

---

3   1 Peter 2:5
4   1 Peter 2:6

there in the living room knew Jesus as their Saviour. But when they experienced the warm fellowship and were able to see the spiritual gifts in operation, something happened within them. Two of them ended up receiving Jesus that night.

Two weeks later we met up again in the same home, but this time there were even more people in the living room. The rumors had spread and people were excited. The sermon that evening had ignited hope. The spiritual gifts had begun to function among us, and God's power was seen in our midst. The things that happened that evening also happened in the gatherings that followed: God met people in many different areas of their lives.

Jesus' body had begun to function. As the first year drew to a close, we could look back on a "year of the Lord's favor" with gratefulness. Together we had experienced the Spirit of the Lord, and many had received the good news that we had been anointed to preach.

The living room became too small. Today that church gathers in a larger building. But it's not the building that is the church. The church is the body, the body of Christ.

The Goal is Always People

When the disciples were filled with the Holy Spirit at Pentecost, something happened to them. Not only did they speak in a different language "as the Holy Spirit gave them this ability",[5] but the room in which they gathered suddenly began to feel too small. They just had to get out! So they left the security of their little fellowship and went out to the streets of Jerusalem to where the people were.

When we live filled with the Spirit, he will lead us to people. The goal is always people. This is why Jesus gave us his Spirit, so that we might be his witnesses. "But you will receive power when the Holy Spirit comes upon you. *And you will be my witnesses*, telling people about me everywhere – in Jerusalem, throughout Judea, in Samaria, and to the ends of the earth."[6]

On the day of Pentecost people "from every nation living in Jerusalem,"[7] heard the testimony of Jesus.

The Holy Spirit communicates with people regardless of their history, language, or culture.

The Holy Spirit communicates with people regardless of their history, language, or culture. He wants to touch, convict, heal, restore and set free. He wants to do this through you and me – the church, his body.

To be filled with the Holy Spirit is of course important for your personal walk with God. But it is equally important to be filled with his Spirit because of the people you meet every day.

---

5   Acts 2:4
6   Acts 1:8
7   Acts 2:5

The mission you have been given is greater than you. You've been given the Holy Spirit for more reasons than for your own benefit. I have often prayed "Holy Spirit, give me more of you!" The Holy Spirit turns that prayer upside down: "Arne, give me more of you!" There is a great difference between us receiving the Holy Spirit and him getting all of us. That was the last thing that happened at Pentecost. The disciples had already been given the Holy Spirit, when the resurrected Jesus stood up and said "receive the Holy Spirit."[8] Fifty days later they received what the "Father had promised,"[9] when they were baptized in the Holy Spirit in Jerusalem.

It says that "the Holy Spirit filled the house"[10] – not only the room they were in, but the whole house, *their whole lives*. There were no longer any rooms in the disciples' lives that were closed off to the Holy Spirit, no signs announcing, "PRIVATE! NO ENTRY!" Jesus filled the whole house with his resurrection life.

The Holy Spirit Convicts People of Sin

After Peter had been filled with the Holy Spirit, he stood up and addressed a crowd of devout Jews "from every nation living in Jerusalem."[11] He led them through the Scriptures and showed them how all the promises are fulfilled in Jesus. He concluded by telling them that "God has made this Jesus,

---

8   John 20:22
9   Acts 1:4b
10   Acts 2:2b
11   Acts 2:5

whom you crucified, to be both Lord and Messiah!"[12]

As Peter said this, something happened to the people listening. The message "pierced their hearts." They were convicted of their sins, and they asked Peter and the other disciples: "What shall we do, brothers?"

Consider this for a moment: What would have happened if Peter had made this speech one day earlier? The same speech, word for word, on the day before Pentecost. What would have happened?

Not too much. It wasn't Peter's convincing arguments that "pierced the hearts" of those who were listening. It was the Holy Spirit that convicted them of their sin.

The Holy Spirit does the same thing today. Convicting people of their sin is his business, not ours.

Convicting people of their sin is his business, not ours.

Still, I must admit that I have at times tried to help him. I have been rather unsuccessful. The only thing I managed to convict people of is that there is no point in continuing the conversation with Arne Skagen.

A woman in England told me that she had spoken with a

---

12 Acts 2:36

psychic who had told her that she could expect five dreadful years. Two weeks later, while the woman and her husband were eating their dinner at a restaurant, one of the light fixtures fell down from the ceiling and hit her husband on the head. He was badly injured and was in a coma for several weeks. Due to the accident, the man lost his job, and in the aftermath had one complication after another.

We sat a long while there in her living room – my friend and I – and listened to this distraught woman. When she was finally done telling her story, she looked at us with anticipation and we shared with her about Jesus. "We believe that he will make a difference in your life," I told her. The woman immediately replied: "I believe in Krishna. That has to be good enough."

I did not give up. My appetite had been whetted, so I tried various ways to convince this woman that Jesus was unique, and that he had the power to set her free.

I got nowhere, however. It felt like I was preaching to deaf ears. We moved from the living room to the kitchen as the woman began to make us some tea. Around the kitchen table with our cups of tea, we continued our conversation and I got more and more frustrated. My attempts to convince her did not seem to get anywhere. The conversation became more of an argumentative discussion. The compassion I had felt for her in the beginning of our conversation was beginning to evaporate. Inside of me I could feel a desperate cry rising up: "Holy Spirit, help me! I am getting nowhere!"

Quickly I began to realize what the problem was. I realized that I had tried to convince her, not through the power of the Holy Spirit, but through the power of Arne Skagen. I had to pray: "Lord, forgive me. Holy Spirit, do what only you can do." Slowly our conversation began to quicken, and the atmosphere began to feel more open.

And then I began to hear a word deep within me. Was it a name? If so, it was completely unfamiliar to me. But I heard it several times. I finally had to ask the woman if the name meant anything to her.

She nodded. "It is one of our gods, the god of confusion. When we bought this house my mother-in-law dedicated our house to him."

My friend and I looked at each other. I asked the woman if we could pray for her house. She nodded. I prayed that the confusion would leave in the name of Jesus, and that God's peace would rest over this house.

After that the woman looked at us and said:

"Please help me."

"What can we do for you?" I asked. "Tell me how I can receive Jesus and receive forgiveness for my sins."

In my own strength I had tried to convince the woman. That had led nowhere. When I finally gave up and let the Holy

Spirit take over, he convinced the woman that she needed Jesus and forgiveness.

We Are All Witnesses

In the Gospel of John, Jesus tells us that he was sent by his Father to fulfill a mission. He is not just mentioning it in passing – he uses the expression "sent" forty times in the same gospel. Jesus says to the disciples, "As the Father has sent me, so I am sending you."[13]

If you are a disciple of Jesus, it means that you are sent. We are *all* witnesses, whether we are aware of it or not. We witness through what we say and even more through what we do. You might at times have experienced the same thing as I have – that what you do speaks louder than what you say. In other words, it's like saying, "I can't hear what you're saying because your life is speaking so much louder!"

Jesus said quite boldly of himself, "Anyone who has seen me has seen the Father."[14] Jesus showed the world who his Father was through his life. The same thing goes for us. The way I carry out my profession, the way I treat others, the way I manage money and property – all of these things are about winning people to Jesus.

We are not in every situation dependent on hearing God's voice or having a revelation on how we are to be witnesses for Jesus.

---

13 John 20:21
14 John 14: 9

We can simply decide to live as Jesus' witnesses every day – it is a conscious choice. That is the way that the Gospel has spread all around the world – through people who have been moved by Jesus and have shared their lives with others, and who have expressed God's love in word and action. The best training for a disciple is on his knees; to bend down and lift others up.

> *The best training for a disciple is on his knees; to bend down and lift others up.*

A Witness in Word and Action

Thomas grew up in a Christian family that was actively involved in the church. During his teenage years he walked away from both his faith and his church.

As an adult, Thomas met God in a new way. He chose to turn to Jesus and was filled with the Holy Spirit. He blew dust off of the Bible he had kept for years, and started to read it with great curiosity. When he went back to the church he used to be a part of, people began to notice that there was something different about him. Passionately Thomas spoke about people he knew who had not met Jesus yet. Thomas settled into the church again and attended meetings on Sundays. But when the weekends were over, he didn't get discouraged. When a new week begins, he is one of those people who quietly think to themselves: Thank God it's Monday!

Chris is a builder. He is a man of few words. During his work hours he likes to let his tools do the talking. When people eventually begin to hear testimonies about people encountering God's love in Chris' workplace, it has more to do with Chris' practical abilities rather than his ability to preach. Chris goes the extra mile for his customers, and he does it without charging them anything extra. He is generous and hardworking, and he does it for his customers and to the Lord. He starts to meet up with people he gets to know through work, and he begins to build friendships. He doesn't switch into preacher mode when he speaks to people about Jesus; he uses the same language that he would normally use when discussing building material.

Things are happening around Chris: more and more people are receiving Jesus. It happens during the week, at the building site or in his home. The quiet builder is a witness of Jesus wherever he goes. When you are with Chris you quickly notice his secret: he quietly and calmly radiates love and care for other people.

"It's all the work of the Holy Spirit," Chris says about what is going on around him. He adds that he is totally dependent on having a close relationship with the Holy Spirit to live the life that he is living.

Hearing and Doing

It's not exactly controversial to point out, as I have done throughout this chapter, that to be a disciple of Jesus means to be sent. The fact that Jesus uses the expression "sent" forty times in the Gospel of John alone would make people nod in agreement when they hear this. To nod in agreement is something you do with your head. That means that on an intellectual level you understand what it means to be sent. In the parable of Jesus and the fortune teller, there were many people who did just that. They heard the Word of God, and seemingly understood it, but it never took root in their hearts. Those who hear the Word and let it grow deeply into their hearts are those who "hear God's word, cling to it and patiently produce a huge harvest."[15] Those who cherish the Word in their heart do not only give it some intellectual thought. They receive the Word through all five senses, and become one with the Word. It is then that the Word will actually bear fruit. James says it so directly, "But don't just listen to God's word. You must do what it says."[16]

When we let the Word go from our heads to our hearts and from our hearts out to our arms and legs, we will start to see things happen around us. We will see the same things that happened around Jesus: people are set free so that they can live the life that God intended them to live.

Anointed for a Mission

"The Spirit of the Lord is upon [me]," Jesus said in the synagogue in Nazareth when he made Isaiah's words his own. In the same breath he added: "For he has anointed me to bring Good News to the poor."[17] Jesus was anointed for a purpose. With

---

15 Luke 8:15
16 James 1:22
17 Luke 4:18

the anointing came a mission. Jesus was anointed to proclaim and demonstrate that God's kingdom is near. The letter to the Philippians tells us that Jesus who was God "instead, [he] gave up his divine privileges; [he] and took the humble position of a slave."[18] He stepped down and became one of us, apart from one thing: he was without sin. By coming to earth in that way – out of his own free will, he gave up his divine privileges – made Jesus completely dependent on the Holy Spirit. It was only in the power of the Holy Spirit that he could preach with the authority that he did and perform miracles, for "you know that God anointed Jesus of Nazareth with the Holy Spirit and with power and how he went around doing good and healing all who were oppressed by the devil, for God was with him."[19] The same anointing that was on Jesus when he was on earth is available for the church today. Jesus said, "As my Father sent me, I send you." This means that Jesus sends us with the same anointing and the same mission. The anointing gives us access to the Spirit who "teaches you everything you need to know."[20] The mission is for "everyone to be saved and to understand the truth."[21]

The anointing cannot be separated from the mission.

The anointing cannot be separated from the mission. If we separate the two, we will end up with religious activities that are kept alive by human effort. It is true that we might be able

---

18 Phil 2:7
19 Acts 10:38
20 1 John 2:27
21 1 Tim 2:4

to keep that going for years, but we should not be surprised when it does not bear fruit. When we start to co-operate with the Holy Spirit who lives within us our work will start to bear fruit. Cooperating with the Holy Spirit is the theme in the next chapter.

4

Co-operating with the Holy Spirit

The Leading Role Belongs to the Holy Spirit

I write a lot about the Holy Spirit in this book. It is unavoidable: He is the Great Evangelist. The Holy Spirit plays the leading role in gathering the harvest, but he invites us to play supporting roles.

It is really important that we take the time to get to know the Holy Spirit better. Who is he? And what does he want? How does he make himself known? How can we hear the voice of the Spirit?

The question of hearing the voice of the Holy Spirit has often been a topic of discussion. Throughout history there have been many people who have said and done strange things arguing that they heard the voice of the Spirit. Because of this, should we play it safe and take everything that the Holy Spirit says with a grain of salt?

The solution is not to "stifle the Holy Spirit,"[1] but to "test them to see if the spirit they have comes from God."[2] The most important reference point in determining if something is from the Spirit is the Bible, the Word of God. If what we feel the Holy Spirit is saying does not line up with the Word of God, we can safely conclude that it was not the Holy Spirit and move on.

The Bible does not give us any other way of living than letting "the Holy Spirit guide your lives."[3] In Acts we see again and again how the Holy Spirit speaks to the disciples and shows them what to say and do.

The Holy Spirit is a communicating Spirit. Jesus calls him "the Counselor," and this must mean that he counsels through speaking. Jesus says about the Holy Spirit that he "will teach you everything and will remind you everything I have told you."[4] In another scripture he says, "My sheep listen to my voice; I know them and they follow me."[5] This is why this chapter is not bonus material for those who are superspiritual. It is written for ordinary disciples like you and me.

Close Communication

The Holy Spirit came upon Jesus when he was baptized by John in the River Jordan. At that very moment he heard the voice of his Father say, "You are my dearly loved Son, and you bring me great joy."[6]

---

1   1 Thessalonians 5:19
2   1 John 4:1
3   Galatians 5:16
4   John 14:26
5   John 10:27
6   Mark 1:11

Jesus heard these words before he had actually gotten started in his ministry. The Father was not commending him for something he had already done, or bragging about some great thing he accomplished by saying, "Well done, my boy!" Instead, he was confirming his unconditional love for his son.

Our heavenly Father is saying the same thing to us, through the Holy Spirit. *My beloved son. My beloved daughter. You bring me great joy.*

The Father's love establishes a safe border around the communication between you and the Holy Spirit. As a son and daughter, you do not have to strain your neck and listen intently to hear his voice. You can relax and hear your Father's familiar and beloved voice speak to you.

Evangelism is important, but it should never be our first priority. Being followers of Jesus is the most important thing. The fruits of following him are many and varied. One of them is that, as we walk with Jesus, he makes us into fishers of men.[7]

Spend Time in God's Presence

Before old ships left a dock, they had to calibrate the compass. They did this by placing the ship in a certain position based on well-known landmarks. The crew could then know with certainty where north, south, east and west were. With the ship in the right position they then were able to calibrate the

---

7   Matthew 4:19

compass. They could then be certain that they could trust the compass and they would keep a straight course.

In the same way, we need to calibrate according to God's will. This happens when we spend time in God's presence – when we read the Bible, worship God and pray to him, and listen to the Holy Spirit.[8] In our daily lives with so much noise coming at us from every side, this doesn't happen on its own. I have to consciously set aside time to spend alone with God. Sometimes I put on my walking boots and go for a hike in the forest or up in the mountains. Then I am able to talk with God, ask him about things that I wonder about, and spend time thinking and listening. Other times, when I'm at home, I sit myself down in my favorite chair, turn on some quiet music and do the same thing.

I am not recommending any particular method. Jesus often sought out secluded places so that he could be alone with the Father.[9] You have to find your own places and do things in your own way. That is good. The important thing is that you find out what helps you live close to the Father.

But mark this: Our Father is *always* close. *We* are the ones who need to draw close to him.

A Gentle Prompting

Do you remember the visit at the coffee shop that I told you about in the first chapter? A woman and two children had

---

8   Ephesians 5:18-20
9   Mark 6:32

come into the coffee shop where a fellow church leader and I were sitting.

I didn't see something written on the wall in the coffee shop, nor I did not hear a voice from above. I simply felt the gentle promting of God's love for the three people who sat at the table next to us.

The Holy Spirit rarely raises his voice. We will most often recognize it as a gentle prompting deep within. Sometimes the prompting can be strong and almost overwhelming, but most of the time it is quiet and discrete. That's how it was for Elijah when he met God on Mount Horeb. It was not in the storm, in the earthquake or in the fire that God made himself known to him, but in the "sound of a gentle whisper." [10]

This is why we need to train ourselves to hear the voice of the Holy Spirit. We train ourselves up, but we do so with an attitude of obedience to the Holy Spirit. We should always respond like Samuel did: "Speak, Lord, your servant is listening!"

In the beginning this may be difficult. But after awhile you will discover that when you say yes to the promptings of the Holy Spirit the first time, it will be easier to say yes the next time. Your first yes will release the next yes, in a chain reaction of actions out of obedience.

---

10   1 Kings 19:12

Samuel's Response

We hear the voice of God many times without often realizing that he is speaking to us. This is not a new problem; Samuel in the Old Testament struggled with the same thing. His method for knowing if it was God who was speaking is simple but effective, and I use it often.

At a young age Samuel served at the temple in Jerusalem, under the supervision of Eli the priest. One night God called for Samuel. Samuel thought that it was Eli who was calling him, and answered, "Here I am; you called me?" This happened three times. Samuel hears God calling him, but does not realize that it is God. He thinks it was Eli calling him each time.

It is Eli who finally realizes that God is the one who is speaking to Samuel. He instructs the boy in what he should do: "Go back to bed! If he calls you again, answer him: 'Speak Lord, your servant is listening!'"

God calls Samuel one more time, the fourth time that night. That tells us a lot about God's patience. If we don't catch him calling us the first, second or third time, he does not give up. He speaks to us over and over again, to try to get our attention. Notice what happens the fourth time. The key that opens up the communication is the response that Samuel gives when God calls him. Samuel answers: "Speak Lord, your servant is listening!"

What is Samuel doing here? Instead of giving a horizontal

response (to Eli), he gives a vertical response (to God). The voice that he hears is the same one as before, but now he lifts his eyes and his response is directed in a different direction: to God.

In the next moment God begins to speak to him and share his plans with him.

Samuel has taught me an important thing when it comes to hearing God's voice. He has taught me to lift my eyes and give God a response. When I get a thought, I have a choice: I can choose to disregard it as an insignificant thought, or I can choose to give God a response: "God, is this *you*? Are *you* the one speaking to me right now?"

When I get a thought, I try not to overanalyze it. Instead, I give a response to God. If the thought doesn't go away on its own but continues to churn inside of me, I choose to believe that it's from God. Other times the thought just fades away after awhile. Then the matter is clear and I don't use any more time thinking about it.

Just Do it!

I was attending once a Christian conference in Finland. During a break I went outside for some fresh air. In the parking lot there was a woman who was busy texting on her cell phone.

As soon as I saw her, an image popped into my mind: I saw a pair of old running shoes with the Nike logo. What do you do with an image like that? The most tempting thing to do is to write it off right away. "An old pair of Nike running shoes? You gotta be kidding!"

What is the alternative? To muster up some courage and go over to the woman with the cell phone and say something like, "Pardon me, but when I saw you, I had a vision of some old worn out running shoes."

That would hardly be seen as a compliment.

I decided to go with Samuel's response. I said to God: "This seems crazy. But if the pair of old sneakers means something, can you please give me something more?" After awhile I started to think of Nike's slogan, "Just do it!" Now I had an image *and* three words. Should I just saunter over and start talking with the woman?

With hesitation I began to walk in her direction. I did not feel particularly bright at the moment. I did not have the feeling that Isaiah describes about "how beautiful on the mountains are the feet of the messenger who brings the good news."[11]

I coughed. The woman looked up from her cell phone and I said, "I sometimes feel God speak to me. A few minutes ago I felt that he gave me some words that might be for you."

(I often use the word "felt" in these situations. This allows for

---

11   Isaiah 52:7

the fact that it might just be Arne Skagen talking and not God).

I told her about the image of the old running shoes. I said to her: "I started to think about Nike's logo. And I feel that the Lord is saying to you: 'Just do it!'" The next thing I know the woman was jumping up and down with a huge smile on her face along with a series of Finnish words. After awhile she spoke to me in English and explained: She had been dating a Christian man for awhile. This morning he had proposed to her. She was happy, but she also felt a bit puzzled and wondered if this was really God's will for her. This was why she had sent at text message to some friends gathered in another part of Finland. She had asked them to pray for her to have clarity and to know God's will. An now during the break an SMS arrived from her friends that said: "We have prayed to God, and we believe he is saying: 'Just do it!'" Right after this, I had walked over to her and told her: "Just do it!" That was why she had started to jump up and down in pure *ilo* (joy in Finnish).

Take Advantage of the "Mistake Quota"

And then you have those times when you've given God a response, but you're still unsure of what to do next. What do you do then? In those cases there's only one way to find out: You have to act. *Just do it!*

But what if I act and it turns out to be wrong? What if it wasn't God after all?

Well, *so what?* Usually the worst thing that happens is that my pride is hurt (which may actually be good for it). After all, we're only human, and it's human to make mistakes. That is why Jesus gave his disciples a good size "mistake quota". I have made use of it quite often.

I was at a Christian meeting. Towards the end of the meeting there was a time of intercession. I started to pray for a woman. I prayed boldly for health, power and strength. To finish off I prayed that God would bless the child she was carrying. "I pray that everything will go well with the birth when the time is right." The woman opened her eyes: "I'm not pregnant."

I looked around with desperation in my eyes, but found no hole to sink into. I just had to remain standing where I was, give her my deepest apologies and ask for forgiveness. "It's okay", she answered. Then she turned around and left. I am so grateful that I have been given a generous "mistakes quota." The good thing is that you'll need it less and less as you start to recognize the different ways in which the Holy Spirit speaks to us. If we sometimes miss it, it doesn't mean that it keeps people from experiencing God's love. "Love covers a multitude of sins."[12] It also covers many mistakes.

Practice, Practice, Practice!

The Holy Spirit speaks to each and every one of us in different ways. To put it in radio language: The Holy Spirit transmits

---

12 1 Peter 4:8

on different frequencies, customized to your personal receiver. A good prayer to start your day with is this: "Holy Spirit, here I am. I want to co-operate with you today. Speak to me and use me."

With these simple words you make yourself open and available to the Holy Spirit. Have an expectation that he will speak to you, but don't get stressed out about it. God heard your prayer, and he will answer. Cooperating with the Holy Spirit often begins with the small things. Bit by bit he allows you to grow into a larger capacity in how you hear and in your obedience to him. The best places to practice hearing the voice of the Holy Spirit is in the small gatherings where we feel safe, such as with family, friends and in life groups. In those settings we can listen to the Holy Spirit in a relaxed atmosphere, test out our thoughts on each other, and with God's Word act on what we believe the Spirit is showing us.

Once I was visiting a life group. They happened to be practicing hearing God's voice and acting on what they were hearing. We sat around the living room table and talked about people that we knew and felt were open to the Gospel. During our conversations a few names were mentioned.

One of the names was Caroline, a mature lady whom one of the people in the life group knew. We prayed for Caroline and agreed to invite her to the next life group meeting.

A few days later I was teaching at another gathering. The theme there was the same – hearing the voice of the Spirit. I moved around the auditorium while I was teaching. As I passed a girl, the chorus of a famous song popped into my head. It wasn't one of my favorite tunes (quite the opposite). But the chorus was so annoyingly catchy that I could not get it out of my head. This was irritating. Here I was teaching, and suddenly I could not get this stupid song out of my head! Part of the lyrics described a specific place in England. I asked the girl I had just passed, "Tell me, does this song mean anything to you?" "My dad is from that place," she answered. Before I continued on with my teaching, we agreed to pray for the girl's parents. We prayed that they would receive Jesus.

Thursday night the life group met up again. Caroline had accepted the invitation and was sitting with us around the living room table. We had a great night, and we were able to show Caroline the love of God in a natural way. Before the night was over she had decided to receive Jesus. When Caroline told us a bit more about herself, we realized that she was the mother of the girl who had made me think of the famous song. Without us knowing it, we had prayed for Caroline the day before! The answer to our prayers came just 24 hours later!

From this example we can learn three things. First, we should never despise the small beginnings (it all began in a life group where they were practicing hearing the voice of the Spirit). Secondly, we should not limit the way the Holy Spirit speaks (he used an annoying chorus from a famous song). Lastly, we learned how important a warm and inviting fellowship can mean to someone. It was in meeting this fellowship that Caroline made a decision to receive salvation.

A Thought Becomes a Miracle

Jesus was persecuted because he healed a sick man on the Sabbath. To those who persecuted him he said, "My Father is always working, and so am I."[13]

Jesus continued to say: "I tell you the truth; the Son can do nothing by himself. He does only what he sees the Father doing. Whatever the Father does, the Son does."

Everything Jesus did has its origin in the Father. Jesus observed what the Father was doing and brought it down to earth. In this way, he fulfilled the prayer that he had taught the disciples to pray: "May your will be done on earth, as it is in heaven."[14]

Jesus' words about seeing what the Father is doing give another dimension to my everyday life as a disciple. Now that I know the truth of the words that "my Father is always working," I can pray anytime and anywhere for him to show me what he's working on. This makes being a disciple very exciting. What is the Father doing *right now*? And, do I dare act on what he is showing me at this *very moment*?

I was sitting on the couch with my legs spread out on the living room table (in other words: the missus was out). In my relaxed posture I said to God: "If there is anything on your heart, just let me know. As you can see, I'm just sitting here on the couch."

---

13 John 5:17
14 Matthew 6:10

As I was sitting on the couch, I began to think about a young man that I had met six months earlier. A few thoughts came to my mind. Were they my own thoughts or were they God's thoughts? Again I was given a choice: I could either ignore the thoughts or I could act on them.

I chose the last option. I quickly discovered that the man lived abroad. It took a while to find his contact information, but I finally found his telephone number. I dialled it, introduced myself and told him why I had called. I said to him, "I feel that God is calling you, and he wants to use you in a special way."

The man wasn't a Christian, but what I said to him sparked such a response in him (he told me later) that shortly afterwards he dealt with his old life and surrendered to Jesus. Since then, God has used this man to lead many people to faith.

A simple thought can become a miracle when we allow the love of Jesus to be expressed through us practically, and when we do what he asks us to do.

God Speaks Through Dreams

If you sit on the couch with your feet up for too long, the next stop could quickly be dreamland. But this won't keep the Holy Spirit from speaking to you. In the Bible we find several examples of how God spoke to people through dreams. And he still does. Once I was visiting a church in the United States. One night while I was there, I had a dream about a man who walked around to different villages digging for water. When I woke up the next morning, I remembered the dream. I imagined that this could have happened in a country like India. And while I was thinking about the man in the dream, the name Henry came to me.

I did not know a man named Henry in this church, and I had also not heard of a well-drilling project in India. The only thing I could do was to give my Samuel response. I said to God, "If you want me to do anything more than pray, I am available. Use me."

During the Sunday service the following day, while I was sharing the Word of God, a man in the congregation caught my attention. It was the man in my dream!

I stopped preaching and asked the man "Is your name Henry?" He nodded, and I shared my dream with him. Henry told me that he was a well-digger by profession. Lately he had had some thoughts about going to India to help dig some wells in the villages there.

While Henry was sharing these thoughts, I had a vision. I saw a large group of people standing around the well listening to someone preach the Gospel. Many of them received Jesus.

I shared this vision with Henry and the rest of the church. With the help of a friend, Henry was able to raise the money to finance the wells. They travelled to India and began their first well-drilling projects. The day that the first well was opened, thousands of people came from all of the surrounding villages. Henry's Indian colleague, Nick, told those who had come that the well was a gift from God to them. Nick shared the Gospel with all those who had gathered around the well and several of them gave their lives to Jesus.

Henry told me all of this in a recent email. It began in the invisible, in a dream. I did my part, Henry did his, and Nick did his. The result: the Gospel was preached in a village in India, and many people came to faith. Today there are several churches in that area.

A Battle to be Fought

Paul encouraged the Galatians to "Let the Holy Spirit guide your lives!"[15] But he does not promise that it will be a life without opposition or battles.

In the letter to the Ephesians he writes, "For we are not fighting against flesh and blood enemies, but against evil rulers and authorities of the unseen world, against mighty powers in this dark world and against evil spirits in the heavenly places."[16] We have a battle to fight when it comes to the harvest. It is important to note that the battle is not against people, which we sometimes might think. In Matthew 10 and Luke 10, when Jesus instructed the disciples in how they were to relate to people who did not want to receive them or their message,

---

15 Galatians 5:16
16 Ephesians 6:12

he didn't ask the disciples to wage war against them. Instead he tells them to "shake [the household's or town's] dust from your feet as you leave."[17] We are fighting spiritual powers, not people. These spiritual powers "are just the opposite of what the Spirit wants. And the Spirit gives us desires that are the opposite of what the sinful nature desires. These two forces are constantly fighting each other, so you are not free to carry out your good intentions."[18]

Because the obstacles are not human, we also do not fight against them with human means. "We use God's mighty weapons, not worldly weapons, to knock down the strongholds of human reasoning and destroy false arguments. We destroy every proud obstacle that keeps people from knowing God."[19]

It is interesting that in Psalm 23 David writes the following about God: "You prepare a feast for me in the presence of my enemies. You honor me by anointing my head with oil."[20] The first thing that God anoints in front of our enemies is our head. When he anoints our head, it means that he wants us to think his thoughts in all situations that we face and don't let ourselves be limited by our natural mind and our natural way of thinking. God anointed our head so that we will know who we are and what we have. We are new creations,[21] and we have received the Holy Spirit who teaches everything.[22]

---

17 Matthew 10:14
18 Galatians 5:16,17
19 2 Corinthians 10:4
20 Psalm 23:5
21 2 Corinthians 5:17
22 1 John 2:27

The Power of the Holy Spirit

"I tell you the truth, anyone who believes in me will do the same works I have done, and even greater works, because I am going to be with the Father."[23] I am not the one saying this. It is Jesus. All the things he did when he walked on this earth, he will do today. He will do it through us.

> *We are called to live out of the heavenly realities in our neighborhood, at work, in our group of friends. Our feet are planted on earth, but our head is in heaven.*

We are called to live out of the heavenly realities in our neighborhood, at work, in our group of friends. Our feet are planted on earth, but our head is in heaven. We have already heard Peter explain why Jesus could do what he did: "You know that God anointed Jesus of Nazareth with the Holy Spirit and with power. Then Jesus went around doing good and healing all who were oppressed by the devil, for God was with him."[24]

When Jesus asks us to do the same things that he did, this means that we can only do these things in the power of the Holy Spirit. If we try to do it in our own power, it won't work. Merely thinking about it can be discouraging. It can only happen when we allow the power of the Spirit, who lived in Jesus, to fill us, speak to us, lead us and work through us.

---

23 John 14:12
24 Acts 10:38

Once while I was working as a taxi driver in a Norwegian city, a new customer had taken a seat in the back of my taxi.

We hadn't driven very long before I started feeling pain all over my body. The pain I felt was in places I have never had pain before, there was no natural explanation as to why I was suddenly feeling pain in these areas. And it did not decrease, either. The opposite happened, in fact: the pain increased. In great distress I asked God to intervene.

I suddenly heard a quiet voice say, "Arne, it is not your pain."

"Not *my* pain?!" I answered back angrily in my mind. "It is definitely *my* body hurting !"

"It is not your pain, but the pain of the woman sitting in your back seat."

All of a sudden I realized that the Holy Spirit was trying to tell me something. Earlier I had asked him to lead me into situations where I could learn to co-operate with him. Now I found myself exactly in a situation like that. While I was sitting there feeling the pain in my body, I began to think of the number 22, without it meaning anything whatsoever to me. We arrived at her address. I read off the taximeter and she paid. Then I took a chance and said, "This might sound crazy, but I sometimes experience God speaking to me. I am a Christian taxi driver, you see. Would you mind if I asked you a personal question?" The woman nodded.

"Do you often experience pain in your body?" The woman nodded again.

"Is the pain located here, here and here?" I asked as I pointed to the areas on my body where I had felt the pain.

"That's right" she said. "But how can you know this? You don't know me!"

"Is it true that you have had this pain for 22 years?" She thought for a while, and then nodded.

"Would you mind if I prayed for you?" I asked her.

"Not at all," answered the woman.

I prayed for the woman in the back seat, a prayer of healing. The pain soon began to let go. But the greatest miracle was that she gave a positive response to the Gospel. Before she left the taxi she had received Jesus. Awhile later she joined the church that I was a part of.

The World's Best Communicator

You might frown at the story of the taxi, saying: "Quite a unique case." The only reason I share it is to show how creative the Holy Spirit can be in his communication. We would be wise to never limit him, nor think that he only communicates in one particular way. The Holy Spirit speaks in the way he wants, in a thousand different ways. He is the world's best communicator. Trust that he'll speak in a way that you can best understand him – through all of your five senses. The Holy Spirit is called the Counsellor, and he counsels by speaking to every one of us. God has made us all different, and that is why he speaks to us in different ways. Remember that relationships are only as strong as the communication is. I want to encourage you to embark on an exciting journey where you explore how the Holy Spirit speaks to you specifically, and how you can have conversations with him.

Listen to the Holy Spirit so that you might see what the Father is doing. Testify about Jesus. All these things are a way of life. If you let it become a lifestyle, I can promise you an exciting life. Here are some tips for those of you who want to grow in this area, and in this way of living:

Let your time in the Word bring life to you. Fill yourself with God's Word, and let the Word live in you. Pray to God, not only for your own needs, but for other people as well.

Talk to the Holy Spirit. Listen to him. Ask him to lead you into situations where you can get to know him better. Don't be afraid of making mistakes. Don't take yourself too seriously.

Read books. Be inspired by stories about how other people live lives filled with the Holy Spirit.

Seek after fellowship. Spend time with other Christians who live a life filled with the Holy Spirit. Let them lay their hands on you and pray for you.

Have expectations. Expect that God will speak to you and use you as his outstretched arm.

Be obedient. If you are not obedient and act on what the Holy Spirit asks you to do, nothing will happen. Never let fear tell you what to do, but listen to the Holy Spirit.

5

Understanding Harvest Language

A "God-Incidence" at a Coffee Shop

I was at a coffee shop (I am not there every day; this book just makes it seem that way). I was standing in line to pay when an elderly man came over to me. He asked me if I could help him carry his tray with tea and cookies over to his table.

"Of course I can," I answered and left the queue.

"Thank you so much for your help," the man replied as I put the tray down at his table. "Have a nice day."

"The same to you," I answered him as I started to look around for the people I was meant to meet – a few of my Christian friends. I saw them out of the corner of my eye, sitting in one of the corners of the café. They waved me over. From where we were sitting I could see the elderly man.

"Why did he approach me, out of everyone here, to help him?" I asked myself. "There are a lot of other people here that he could have asked just as easily."

I quickly corrected myself: "Relax. Take it easy. Don't make this into something more than it is – simply one of life's many coincidences."

But my walk with the Holy Spirit has weakened my faith in coincidences. Instead, I have started to believe more and more in "God-incidence;" that is, meetings and situations that God has beforehand "put in place so that we would walk in them."

"Pardon me for a moment," I told my friends as I stood up and walked over to the elderly man. He was still sitting on his own.

"Is it okay if I sit with you?" I asked.

The man looked up. He nodded and smiled. We had a nice chat. The man was approaching 90 and had many stories to tell from his long career in the military. While the memories were flooding his mind, a few thoughts hit me. They were about loneliness and emptiness.

After he had told me about his military career, he started to share a bit about his family. His wife had died several years before; his children all lived abroad. In what had once been a large circle of friends, he was soon the only one still alive.

"How do you feel about that?" I asked him.

The man lowered his face and looked at the table.

"A bit empty. At times I feel very lonely and abandoned."

"God knows your situation," I told him. "He can even help you break free from the loneliness."

God was now the topic of our conversation, but the man did not seem to mind, showing just as much interest in the conversation as he had earlier. When I asked him if he wanted to receive Jesus and make peace with God, he answered simply: "Yes, I would like that."

Afterwards we exchanged addresses and phone numbers. One of my friends there that day is a pastor in the local area. He promised me that he would followup the man and help him become a disciple of Jesus.

The Harvest Speaks

The harvest is ripe. We established that in Chapter Two. Now we are going to discover that the harvest has a *language*. The harvest sends out signals; it speaks. If we can learn how to recognize harvest language, I am convinced that we as individuals and churches will experience a breakthrough in seeing people receiving Jesus.

The Bible tells us that God has put eternity into the human heart.1 Every human being is carrying a longing in their hearts for eternity – for God. But not everyone knows that God is

---

1   Ecclesiastes 3:11

the one they're longing for. To fill this void many resort to rituals, alternative ideologies, healing, angel schools and many other things. Many are sincere in their quest; they truly want to figure out the meaning of life. There is no reason for Christians to raise their eyebrows at this sincere quest.

The longing for eternity that God has placed in every human heart has to be expressed. It is seeking a language. But it rarely speaks in big letters. Many times it does not even use words at all. Still, the harvest language can be heard by those who have an ear to listen.

Do you remember the chat you had with your colleague at work when he shared some personal things with you? Or the neighbor who told you that she has been ill? The phone call you've been thinking of making to encourage a distant family member who has been placed in a nursing home? The fellow student who nonchalantly told you that he often feels lonely and abandoned in this world?

All of these could be harvest language. The reason why people send out these signals when they are with you is because you have the answer on the inside: Jesus Christ – who calls himself "the way, the truth and the life."[2]

"But what if I can't hear the harvest language," you might object.

---

2   John 14:6

"What if I act on what I feel, and then discover that it was wrong?"

I would turn that around and say: "What if it is right! What if it really is the harvest language you're hearing?" As long as you are yourself, and as long as you are conveying Jesus' love and care in a sincere way, people will get a glimpse of Jesus anyway. "I hear that you are having a difficult time right now. Is there anything I can do for you?" A simple sentence might be the start of the conversation that leads to the salvation of one person. "I have prayed for you lately, and I want you to know that God sees you and cares about you." Warm and sincere words that build a bridge between you and the other person, a bridge that God's love can walk over.

Jesus Understood Harvest Language

Jesus understood the harvest language better than anyone. His "language ear" was so well-tuned that it could detect the difference between genuine harvest language and harvest language that wasn't quite as sincere.

Picture a rich, young man approaching you and asking: "What good things can I do to get eternal life?" What would you think? I would have thought "harvest language! Ripe harvest! Give me the scythe!" A rich young man came to Jesus and asked him that question. Jesus countered him with another question: "Why do you ask me about what is good? There is only one who is good. But if you want to gain life, keep my commands!"[3] As the story unfolds it becomes apparent that the rich young man is only committed to a certain point – until they talk about money. When Jesus puts his finger on this sensitive area, the man walks away discouraged. At first sight he appeared to be "ripe harvest," when in reality he wasn't.

Zacchaeus was also wealthy, very wealthy.[4] As a tax collector for the occupying powers he had made himself wealthy at the cost of his fellow countrymen. In contrast to the rich young man there was nothing about Zacchaeus that would imply that he was ripe for the harvest. He placed himself on the sidelines of all the commotion that was going on when Jesus came to Jericho. From a distance, from a high branch, he observed all the commotion happening around the carpenter's son from Nazareth.

Who knows what's going on behind people's façade? Here we are often mistaken. We are blinded by the outer things and draw hasty conclusions.

Jesus does not do this. He looks past the outer appearance, he observes what is going on – on the inside. During that day in Jericho, he lifted his gaze and looked out on the crowd, and he saw ripe harvest in the sycamore tree.

What is it that made Zacchaeus forget his dignity as a wealthy man, and climb like a boy up into the tree?

---

3   Matthew 19:17
4   Luke 19:1-10

Body language can also be harvest language. With his short-statured body up in the tree, Zacchaeus said without using words: "See me. See my loneliness, my poverty amidst all my wealth."

In Norway were I live, we are surrounded by wealth, and I believe that we are surrounded by people like Zacchaeus. Do we see them? Do we notice the subtle signals they send out? Do we hear the inaudible harvest language?

A People of Peace

When Jesus asked Zacchaeus to come down from the tree, the tax collector reacted in the following way: "He hurried down and received him with joy."

That is how people of peace react. They receive Jesus with joy. They listen to what Jesus has to say. They receive the new life that Jesus offers. Our job is not to shake people down from the trees against their own will. We are called to go to those who are already longing for Jesus, even if they themselves aren't conscious of this longing.

In Luke 10 Jesus sends out his disciples "to every place and every city that he himself was going to visit." Before he sends the disciples out two by two, he gives clear instructions as to the people they are meant to spend their time on: "When you enter a house, first say, 'Peace to this house.' If someone who promotes peace is there, your peace will rest on them; if not, it will return to you."[5]

---

5   Luke 10:5,6

As Jesus' disciples we are to carry out "prayer and thanksgiving for all people." But the people that we are to spend most of our time on are those that Jesus calls "people of peace." [6] These are people who receive us with openness and with friendliness. They listen to what we have to tell them, they ask questions with curiosity and respond. These are the people that Jesus asks us to spend the most time on – not on those who only want to debate things or want to win discussions.

There are many of these people of peace. They are everywhere. I can guarantee you that you have them in your network, in your family and at your workplace. It is exciting to think that these people of peace know other people of peace, and that is how the network grows.

I read in a newspaper article that all of us are only 4.74 links away from the rest of the world.[7] This means that a friend of your friend probably knows a friend of anyone in the whole world. The social media has had an impact on how the world has been minimized in this way. When we start to think about friendship evangelism this gives us overwhelming options.

My Favorite Method

The Holy Spirit has many names in the Bible. He is called the Advocate, Guide and Counsellor. These functions are not limited to a few situations, like when we read the Bible or pray

---

6   Luke 10:6
7   *Aftenposten*, 23 November 2011

to God. The Holy Spirit wants to be our advocate, guide and counsellor in all of life's situations, in all of life's areas.

This means that he also wants to be involved in harvesting.

The Holy Spirit is the best evangelist of all.

The Holy Spirit is the best evangelist of all. He sows into people's lives and he harvests. He will give you advice. He will guide you. He knows the people you hang out with better than they know themselves. He knows what they are longing for, and he knows what they need in every waking moment. He has the keys to open closed doors.

It's not always easy to know what harvest language is, and what it is not. Fortunately I can always ask the Holy Spirit. This is my favorite method when it comes to evangelism, the only method I believe in: Ask the Holy Spirit!

Get out a pen and paper. Write your name down on the sheet, and draw a circle around it. Outside of your own circle, draw more circles.

Sit back and relax. Ask the Holy Spirit to go on a journey with you through all of your networks, starting with the people you know well, to people you know more formally. Ask the Spirit to tell you what he sees – what is happening in your network. Listen to him and talk to him about what he is showing you. When he reminds you of a name (when a name appears in your thoughts), write it down in one of the empty circles on the sheet.

After awhile you begin to draw lines between the circles; some of those who know you also know each other.

Do you see it? Your network is filled with people of peace. You are surrounded by a ripe harvest.

What you have drawn here is only your network. Imagine if everyone in your church or in the life group sat down and drew up similar maps of their networks. We would soon get a glimpse of a greater harvest. Then we could put the maps together and talk about how we affect each other's networks. We could start to pray for one another's friends.

This is not just an idea that I'm introducing here – it is the theme of the last chapter of the book: "Harvesting Together."

Everyone Can Learn to Recognize Harvest Language

When I teach about harvest language in a church, I often have people come over to me afterwards and ask: "What you're telling us is exciting. But does it work in practice? Can anyone learn to recognize harvest language? Can I learn to recognize it?

Behind the question there is the unspoken belief: "You are an 'evangelist.' You have a special gift that lets you recognize harvest language. It is not a problem for you. But there are different spiritual gifts and ministries, and all of us are not evangelists. And this is why not everyone can recognize harvest language."

The Bible does tell us quite accurately that there is a difference between spiritual gifts and acts of service. Paul highlights this: "A spiritual gift is given to each of us so we can help each other."[8] He also reminds us that the purpose of the gifts is to "to equip God's people to do his work and build up the church, the body of Christ."[9]

In other words, it is not only the evangelists that are to do the harvesting, but the whole church body. The primary role of the evangelist is to equip "the holy ones" – you and I, to do the job. When the resurrected Jesus said "You will be my witnesses," he was not talking to a group of specially equipped evangelists. He was talking to the whole group of disciples, each with different gifts and abilities. Jesus said: "You will be my witnesses."[10]

We are all called to testify about Jesus, regardless of our abilities and giftings. We can all learn to recognize the harvest language. We have all received the Holy Spirit, and he is the evangelist with a capital E.

After a seminar a woman came over to me and asked me a question like the one I just referred to: "Does this work in practice? Can I learn to recognize harvest language?"

A few days later the woman called her cable company to cancel some channels that she no longer wanted. She let them know which channels she wanted to cancel and which ones to keep.

---

8   1 Corinthians 12:7
9   Ephesians 4:12
10   Acts 1:8

Among the channels she wanted to keep was the God Channel. When she mentioned the Christian TV channel, the customer service rep replied: "I am a Hindu." This information came out of nowhere, like a bolt of lightning. Just as suddenly a thought hit her: "Harvest language! This must be the harvest language that I heard about in that seminar! Why else would he tell me that he is a Hindu?"

The woman answered: "I am a Christian." Then she tells him, in a few sentences, what her friendship with Jesus means to her. Joy. Peace. A future. Hope.

"I need what you have," replied the customer service rep.

"You can have it, all you have to do is to say yes to Jesus," the woman answered. She added: "You can receive Jesus at any moment, anywhere. Even over the phone, if you'd like."

"I would like that," replied the customer service rep.

Phases in Harvesting

Harvest work moves through different phases in a cycle. In this book I am putting the most emphasis on the harvesting phase, because I feel that this is where the need for mobilization is the greatest. The harvest really is ready, and this is why many more workers need to be ready. Still, it can be helpful to know a bit more about the other phases in the cycle. "For everything there is a season, a time for every activity under heaven,"[11] says the writer of Ecclesiastes. This also applies to harvest work. There is a time to cultivate, a time to sow, a time to water and a time to harvest.

Let us look a bit more closely at the other phases that occur before the harvesting phase.

Cultivate

In many places throughout my home country of Norway the landscape is marked by stone fences. The fences are made of rocks that the farmers have removed from the earth in order to farm it. This is an example of cultivation.

In Genesis a picture is painted of a field where not a single piece of grass has grown forth yet. The reason was that God had not let it rain on earth and "there were no people to cultivate the soil."[12]

When we as harvest workers cultivate, it means that we remove the stumbling blocks for those around us. Some of the most common stumbling blocks are bad experiences with Christians, feeling judged, prejudices, misunderstandings and a lack of knowledge. When people get to know Christians who show them compassion and love, many of these stumbling blocks will disappear on their own.

---

11 Ecclesiastes 3:1
12 Genesis 2:5

I went to visit a young married couple with a buddy of mine. The man had cancer, and we were there to pray for him. Before we started to pray, we asked him what his relationship with God was like. Several stumbling blocks surfaced. During his childhood he had been exposed to propaganda of the type that stated "God is watching you all the time, you better watch out." Recently he had been watching some Christian TV shows that he firmly disapproved of. I had watched some of the same programs and had to admit that I understood why he had every reason to react the way he did.

During our conversation we were able to remove some of the stumbling blocks. At the same time we were able to show God's love to both of them. Slowly but surely, with the help of the Holy Spirit, they began to get a clearer picture of what God is really like. This meant that we could remove the last stumbling blocks, and later on they were both able to receive Jesus.

Sow

"So faith comes from hearing, that is, hearing the Good News about Christ,"[13] Paul writes.

What is the Good News? The news about God's kingdom being near, because of Jesus Christ, and that the kingdom is available to all who want to partake of it.

---

13 Romans 10:17

It is important that faith is expressed through actions, but that of course does not mean that words are insufficient. In his letter to the Romans, Paul asks a rhetorical question: "But how can they call on him to save them unless they believe in him? And how can they believe in him if they have never heard about him? And how can they hear about him unless someone tells them?"[14] The Gospel has to be communicated with words in order for most people to understand.

Therefore, use God's Word actively. Send it out as a text message, put it on Facebook. Read the Bible with friends who are curious about it. Practice telling the story of Jesus in your own words. Be prepared to also share your personal story of how you came to be a friend of Jesus. Don't hold anything back: "Whoever sows sparingly will reap sparingly, and whoever sows generously will also reap generously." If you are uncertain of what God's Word can do, take a deep breath and read what Isaiah wrote: "The rain and snow come down from the heavens and stay on the ground to water the earth. They cause the grain to grow, producing seed for the farmer and bread for the hungry. It is the same with my Word. I send it out, and it always produces fruit. It will accomplish all I want it to, and it will prosper everywhere I send it."[15] Also notice that Jesus has already prayed for the people you share the Gospel with: "I am praying not only for these disciples, but also for all who will ever believe in me through their message".[16]

---

14 Romans 10:14
15 Isaiah 55:10
16 John 17:20

Water

To water means to be faithful to the people whom God has entrusted to you. The woman I told you about in the beginning of the book is a good example: Every day for forty years she faithfully prayed for her husband. In the end he came to faith. We water when we tirelessly continue to encourage people, listen to them, bless them and pray for them. All these things help out in supplying the Word that has been sown with good growth conditions. In its time it will grow forth and develop into a ripe harvest, that you, me or others will have the joy of harvesting.

Cultivate, sow, water and harvest: These are the phases in harvesting. Who does what is not so important. God is the only one who brings forth growth: "I planted the seed in your hearts, and Apollos watered it, but it was God who made it grow."17 This verse from the first letter to the Corinthians reminds us of another important thing: Evangelizing is not a solo project. It is done through teamwork where we work together with other people and with God.

We harvest together.

---

17 1 Corinthians 3:6

6

Together in the Harvest

Harvesting is a Team Effort

The life group consisted of seven people. Some of us had just moved to the area, while others had lived there for as long as they could remember and were well established with family, friends and acquaintances.

One night we sat down and drew a map of our social networks. Afterwards we placed our maps next to one another on the living room table. This opened our eyes. We discovered connections and links that we hadn't noticed before. It revealed a great harvest.

We started to pray for one another's friends and acquaintances. We prayed that the Holy Spirit would show us their needs, and how we could meet these needs. Most of what we did was simple, everyday things. We made phone calls just to have a chat; we invited people over for coffee, to the movies and out for fishing.

Just after we had started our life group I met Steve. He had just received Jesus, but did not have anyone following him up. I invited him along to the life group.

One week when the group was gathered at Steve's house, his parents had come for a visit. We established a good connection with them, and they soon joined our life group. We got to know several of Steve's friends. Some joined the life group, where they received Jesus.

Two of these friends were Jennie and Mike. They had large networks that gave us many new contacts. With Jennie and Mike we prayed for Liz and Pete for a period of time. We had been over for coffee at their house several times. Pete came along to a Sunday morning meeting at our church. There he received Jesus (it can happen on Sundays too, you see, even if this book mostly focuses on Mondays). Not long afterwards Liz made the same decision. In Liz and Pete's network several people have given their lives to Jesus.

We have also experienced some of the neighbors coming to faith after one of them had come along to a life group meeting and gotten healed.

The life group started with seven people. As more and more people have been impacted, the network has expanded. After awhile it looked like this:

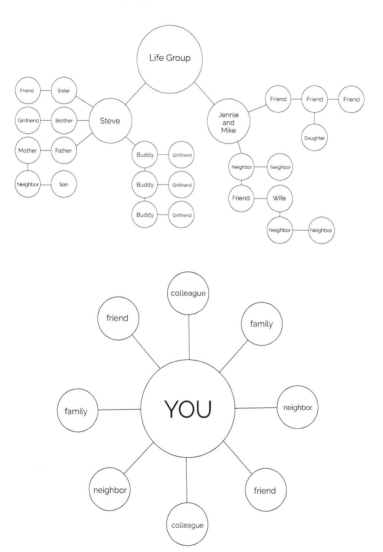

Picture the church that you are a part of and imagine that each person is like the illustration above. They touch someone who touches someone else. A home of peace will inevitably recognise another home of peace. So if you are a part of a life group, cell group, etc. think bigger. If there are 30 of you, think 300.

The key for us in our life group is to work as a team. We harvest together, side by side, and that makes all the difference.
Together we map out our networks.
Together we pray for one another's contacts.
Together we serve people with our different personalities and giftings.
Together we win people's trust.
Together we build friendships.
Together we welcome new people into the fellowship.
Together we see new people come to faith.
Together we help new Christians become disciples of Jesus.

Not everyone that we pray for has received Jesus. So we learn a lesson of faithfulness and patience. Several of the people we prayed for and built friendships with didn't come to faith until many years later.

God-Given Limitations

When people meet Christians individually, they only get a small glimpse of Jesus. When they meet us as a fellowship, they have the opportunity to discover more of Jesus and experience more of his love. It's when we stand together that both they and we are able to understand "how wide, how long, how high, and how deep his love is. May you experience the love of Christ, though it is too great to understand fully."[1]

Have you ever been annoyed at your own limitations? Have you ever fallen victim to the temptation of comparing yourself with others? If only I had his courage, or her talent. If I only had her knowledge, or had his social skills."

Comparison only creates pride (if you think that you score higher than the other person) or discouragement (if you feel that you fall short). Both of these are bitter fruits that don't come from the Holy Spirit. Rejoice in your limitations!

Rejoice in your limitations!

The fact that you cannot do everything, know everything or have all the spiritual gifts has a simple explanation: God wants it to be that way. He has created you with limitations for one reason: He wants you to honor him in all you do alongside others.

To the church in Corinth, where there were individuals who were blinded by their own excellence, Paul writes: "How strange a body would be if it had only one part! Yes, there are many parts, but only one body. The eye can never say to the hand: 'I don't need you.' The head can't say to the feet, 'I don't need you.' In fact, some parts of the body that seem to be the

---

1   Ephesians 3:18,19

weakest and least important are actually the most necessary. […] All of you together are Christ's body, and each of you is a part of it."[2]

When we work together, we help each other with the things we're good at, what we have been given a measure of grace to do. Who does what is not important. Paul writes that it is the Holy Spirit "who distributes all these gifts. He alone decides which gift each person should have."[3]

It is the Spirit's gifts, not ours. The gifts are tools. The Holy Spirit uses them to fulfill his purposes here on earth. He uses the gifts when he wants and wherever he wants, and he uses whoever he wants. All we need to do is to be available so that God's power can flow through us to accomplish what he wants. Instead of focusing on the gift, focus on the Giver and what he wants. In all he does, the Holy Spirit points to Jesus and exalts him.

The important thing is not "who does what," but that each person does what the Holy Spirit asks him or her to do. Some are really good at seeing other people, and some are great comedians who spread joy and laughter wherever they go. Others have the ability to listen and ask timely questions.

Time after time I have seen the interaction between the different personalities and giftings unfold within the fellowship. It is just as fascinating every time it happens.

---

2   1 Corinthians 12:19-22, 27
3   1 Corinthians 12:11

It All Started On The Ferry

Andrew is sitting on the ferry, on his way out to a small island. A group of friends just sat down at the table next to him. Their conversation becomes loud and intense. It's not hard to catch what they're talking about because God and Jesus are mentioned in about every other sentence.

Andrew gets curious, so he discretely listens in on the conversation. At first nobody notices him, but soon they discover that they have an audience. They turn to Andrew and start talking with him. At first Andrew is a bit bothered by it, but he is quickly immersed in the conversation and the fellowship.

As the ferry arrives at the docks they ask Andrew if he would like to come to a gathering in the home of some Christians that night.

Andrew is busy that night, but he does come the following week. He receives a warm welcome, and the welcome and hospitality does something to Andrew. He returns the following week and brings his friend Justin with him.

At the end of the evening Andrew is asked if he wants to receive Jesus. The thought is not foreign to him, but he answers: "I'll wait till Monday. That way I can go to parties and get drunk during the weekend."

"It's up to you," says Josh, one of the leaders of the life group.

"You do as you please."

Quietly, in his own mind, Andrew begins to reflect on what he wants to do. Finally he realizes that there's no good reason to postpone it any longer, not even till Monday.

"I might as well receive Jesus tonight," says Andrew.

His buddy Justin says the same thing.

It Continued on Land

Over the next few months Josh spends a lot of time with Andrew. Sometimes he drops by with a freshly made take-away pizza under his arm. A friendship begins to grow. For Josh it is a joy to see how Andrew's life has begun to change since he received Christ.

Someone else who notices this change is Mark, a previous colleague of Andrew's.

"I remember Andrew as being someone who thought he was something special. At the work parties he would always cause trouble."

Since he became a Christian Andrew seems different. His sense of humour is the same, but he is less boastful than he used to be. Mark thinks he seems to be more humble.

His previous colleagues resume contact with Andrew. What Mark doesn't know is that Andrew has decided that he wants to win him for Jesus. He starts to pray for him, and when he gets an opportunity he invites him along to the Christian fellowship.

"My plan failed to succeed," Andrew says. "Some of the other people in the fellowship beat me to the punch. They invited Mark to a gathering where he received Jesus. Mark was saved before we resumed contact. So I had to become his friend afterwards."

Someone else who notices a change in Mark's life is his cousin Eric.

"What made me curious was the big difference before and after Mark became a Christian. I also wasn't doing so well at that time. So I asked Mark if Jesus could help me too."

Mark says yes without any hesitation. Eric decides to get to know Mark's Christian friends. During worship night Eric is met by God. That night he receives Jesus.

Andrew, Mark and Eric are now passionate about seeing more of their friends find Jesus. So they pray for them, invite them over to their place, go bowling and go to the movies.

"We've seen several of our buddies get saved. It hasn't stopped. It just keeps happening," Mark says.

Luke 10: Work Instructions

Luke 10:1-12 is the closest we get to a job description for harvest workers in the Bible. We've already looked at much of what Jesus talks about in this Bible passage:

- The harvest is so great and so close, that it's touching the tips of our shoes.
- The workers are so few, but their numbers will grow when ordinary disciples understand that harvesting is for everyone.
- We are to go to people of peace, greet them and stay with them.
- A harvesting team consists of a minimum of two disciples that Jesus sends out together.

So far I have only quoted fragments of Luke 10. I feel a bit bad about that. Here is the passage in its entirety.

Read it. Learn from it. Live it.

"The Lord now chose 72 other disciples and sent them ahead in pairs to all the towns and places he planned to visit. These were his instructions to them: "The harvest is great, but the workers are few. So pray to the Lord who is in charge of the harvest; ask him to send more workers into his fields. Now go, and remember that I am sending you out as lambs among wolves. Don't take any money with you, or a traveler's bag, or an extra pair of sandals. And don't stop to greet anyone on the road. Whenever you enter someone's home, first say: 'May God's peace be on this house.' If those who live there are peaceful, the blessing will stand; if they are not, the blessing will return to you. Don't move around from home to home. Stay in one place, eating and drinking what they provide. Don't hesitate to accept hospitality, because those who work deserve their pay. If you enter a town and it welcomes you, eat whatever is set before you. Heal the sick, and tell them, 'The Kingdom of God is near you now.' But if a town refuses to welcome you, go out into its streets and say, 'We wipe even the dust of your town from our feet to show that we have abandoned you to your fate. And know this –the Kingdom of God is near!' I assure you; even wicked Sodom will be better off than such a town on judgment day."

(Luke 10, 1-12. You can also read the parallel text in Matthew 10)

Identify the Networks

For several years now I have been able to help churches with harvesting. The churches, different as they may be, have all had a collective experience: When they start to examine the networks of the members in the church more closely, doors begin to open everywhere. The process of outlining the social networks opens the eyes of many churches.

We always start by asking: Who are the people in your network? Which people do you feel are positive towards you and what you believe? Who listens when you share with them about your faith, and who asks inquiring questions? Who knocks on your door when they need help and who comes to you with their personal problems?

In other words, in the words of Jesus in Luke 10: Who are the people of peace in your network?

In the identification phase (just like the other phases of harvesting) we are dependent on the Holy Spirit for guidance and advice. He knows your network better than you do. He knows what's going on inside the people you know.

When the members of the church have spent time thinking and praying and the Holy Spirit has spoken, we ask them to get a sheet of paper and draw their networks.

A simple drawing of "your network of people of peace" can look similar to the drawing on page 81. When you put your drawing next to someone else's drawing in your church, you will discover something exciting: There are connecting points and links between the networks! Some of the people in your network are also in my network. That means that we can work together. We can pray for one another's friends and make creative plans of how we can affect each other's network.

This sounds great, doesn't it? At least it does on paper, in *theory*. But does it work in *practice*?

One Week in November

In the 1980's there was a church planted in the United Kingdom. Right from the start the church had a clear vision to touch the city and the surrounding community with God's love. During the first years the church grew as new people came to faith. A few years later the church had a few hundred members. A lot of good things were happening in the church, and the activities were thriving. Yet the clear focus of making an impact on the city and its people with the love of God had started to decline. It happened unnoticeably, without anyone in the church intending for it to happen.

It was still a great and active church, just a bit less outward-looking than it had been at the start. This is the way it has been for the past ten years. Are people in the church content with that? When they sit down and talk about it, it becomes obvious that they're not content at all with the situation. They realize that there has been too much "internal maintenance" over the last few years, and that this has come at the expense of what they really want and of their vision: to see people in their community come to faith in Jesus and become his disciples.

I met the church for the first time a year and a half ago. They invited me there to teach on harvesting. We spent the weekend together and spent most of our time looking at the members' social networks. When asked about who they felt were responding well to them and to what they believe, lots of names were mentioned.

I have seen this happen many times in several churches: When we talk about harvesting, we automatically begin to think about campaigns, strategies and methods. These things may be effective, but I would rather talk about *people*. Why? Because we can't see the people for the harvest! We don't hear the harvest speak to us, seven days a week, starting Monday morning. Yet we *overhear* the harvest language from people who are positive to us and share their challenges and problems with us.

The first weekend with the church we mainly talked about people. We talked about them and prayed for them. At the end of the weekend I challenged the members of the church to spend time with these people. Build friendships with them, invite them over, include them and bless them in concrete and creative ways.

I recently revisited the church. It was encouraging to notice the enthusiasm and expectation that characterized the church. We were going to spend a week together, a week in the harvest field, meeting with people that were ripe for the harvest.

SUNDAY

A student had invited a fellow student to the morning service at the church. Someone else had called someone who hadn't come to church in over ten years. A mother had asked her daughter if she wanted to come along. All three receive Jesus.

MONDAY

A couple in the church invite a couple they know to a coffee shop. She had been to a few meetings in the church, and he had never wanted to set foot in a church building his hole life. Now the church comes to him instead. In the coffee shop, during a relaxed conversation with friends, both are met with the love of

God. Then and there they both receive Jesus.

In the evening a couple from church that run an antique shop invites us to their home. Several of their customers are into alternative spirituality: healing, crystals, energies, etc. The couple invites some of them to their home this Monday night. We have exciting conversations about life's great questions. The customers from the antique shop are really open for us to pray for them. When we do, they experience God's presence and power in a way they had never felt before. All three receive Christ.

TUESDAY

Some students in the church have arranged an Alpha Course at the university in town. It's held in a student apartment on campus, during one of the free periods in the middle of the day. One of the participants of the Alpha Course receives Jesus. That evening we were at a married couple's home – friends of someone in the church. He is a Christian, she is not. Not until this Tuesday night.

WEDNESDAY

We are at a prayer meeting in the church building. We pray and ask God for the city and its citizens. While we're praying a man passes by outside on the sidewalk. He is going to London today, to meet with a spiritualist and fortune-teller. He sees a man entering the church building and feels drawn to him. The man, who is the pastor of the church, asks him if he wants to come along. Once in the building he experiences the presence of God's love. He also overhears a sentence that is spoken by someone in the building: "There is only one way to God: Jesus Christ." The man immediately answers: "Jesus, come into my life."

THURSDAY

We are back at the coffee shop. Someone in the church has invited a friend they haven't seen in awhile. As we are talking about God he is filled with the Holy Spirit and begins to speak in tongues. The same thing happens to a woman we meet later on.

In the evening we meet with another friend of someone in the church. The man works as a bouncer and he looks like one. He's a tough guy, but God proves to be tougher. The bouncer hears the Gospel that is "the power of God at work, saving everyone who believes."4 The bouncer believes.

FRIDAY

On Friday we visit a Christian couple that lives in a different part of the city. They're going through some hard times, so they really appreciate the visit. We pray together and encourage them. They want to stand together with the church to reach out to people in their part of the city.

SATURDAY

We spend the afternoon in the home of a couple from the

---

4   Romans 1:16

church who have invited their whole family. Many of them want to be prayed for. Two of them receive Jesus.

SUNDAY

A young girl receives Jesus during the Sunday meeting.

That night the church puts on a big celebration. With the exception of two people, everyone who was saved during the week comes to the party. Many of them bring their families, friends and colleagues. It is powerful to see and hear them get up and share what has happened to them.

It is also powerful for one of the husbands of the women that share. When he hears his wife's testimony, he decides that he too wants to receive Jesus.

A few months later I speak with the pastor on the phone. He tells me that all these people are actively involved in the church. He adds: "We are still leading new people to Jesus."

Three Weeks in June

A church that I visited in England had about 250 members. The church has had a steady, but slow growth for quite a few years.

In 2007 the church started to focus on bringing the harvest in from the city. The members came together to practice sharing the Gospel along with their personal testimonies. They were taught how to recognize the voice of the Spirit and how to pray for other people. During the meetings at the church they set aside plenty of time for testimonies from people who had shared the Gospel with someone or prayed for the sick.

My task was to help them identify the natural networks people in the church had. I asked them: "Who do you feel the Holy Spirit is talking to you about in your circle of friends? Do you know anyone who needs to be touched by God's power?"

Many other questions were asked to help people open their eyes to the harvest that is out there waiting. People were encouraged to be creative and ask God to show them new ways that they could get in touch with people. People are different, and this means that we need to find different ways of reaching out so that we can reach many.

We prepared ourselves for the fact that the Holy Spirit was not likely to blow the harvest into the church building. We realized that it was more likely that the Holy Spirit would be sending us out of the church building, out to the awaiting harvest.

In June of 2008 we planned a week where members were to take the initiative to contact those they felt God had reminded them of during the "identification of networks" phase. They called friends and neighbours. They invited them for breakfast, lunch, dinner, cakes and coffee, even meals and a late night snack. There were barbeque parties, cheese parties and other parties. Creativity was flowing, and a lot of headway was made. The members of the church got involved in each other's networks and used one another's giftings and abilities across the board. It soon became apparent that this was an important catalyst for what happened later.

For the next three weeks the church saw four to five people receive Jesus every day. Some were healed of their sicknesses and others from drug addictions. During the month of June many of the people in the church saw their friends, neighbors and colleagues come to faith. Many of these were people they had prayed for over a longer period of time, without realizing the fact that they were ripe for the harvest.

Others began working among refugees and immigrants. They gave their new fellow citizens practical help in their everyday lives: They helped them fill out official papers and helped them with their English acquisition. Every week they had their own gatherings where many received Jesus. The key was the practical love they experienced from the people in the church.

Now to the crucial question: Is everyone who received Jesus in 2008 still a part of the church? The answer to that is truthfully no. *Only three out of four* of them are active members in the church. One of the most important explanations to the fact that so many are still attending church is the strength of the personal relationships within the church. It is crucial that the discipling of the new Christians starts from day one.

Does this church still see the same growth now as they did in 2008? They do not see as much as they did then, but they do see people come to faith weekly. They themselves say that there has been a paradigm shift. They have started to think and act in a new way.

It all started with the fact that the church took Jesus' instructions in Luke 10 seriously. By focusing on the people of peace, they got in touch with people that Jesus "himself would have visited." Jesus had planned to visit them, but he sent the people of the church ahead. Jesus came right after, with salvation, restoration and new life.

I usually put it like this: When we go, he comes.

Thank God it's Monday

In this book I have shared some stories, and I have shared the most important things that I have learned after a few decades of being a harvest worker. Are you ready for a summary?

1. The driving force is God's love. God loves people: you and everyone else.
2. The harvest is ready. You and I are surrounded by it.
3. Jesus sends us. You belong to a sent group of people.
4. The Holy Spirit fills us and leads us. He has the leading role, and he is in control.
5. The harvest speaks, but rarely with a loud voice. Use your eyes and your ears!
6. Harvesting is a team effort. We are much stronger when we stand together.

Thank you for journeying with me through the book. I am convinced that you and your friends have an exciting voyage ahead of you, a voyage that will give you many new friends, and that will give Jesus many new followers.

Thank God it's Monday. Jesus says: "Now go!"[5]

---

5   Luke 10:3

Appendix:
Recommended Harvesting Strategies

1. The 'Identifying Networks' Phase

Get an overview of the connections you have with people who are positive towards you, meaning "women and men of peace" (Chapter 5).

Ask the Holy Spirit to show you who is open to the Gospel, and who is close to making a decision. Be prepared for a surprise or two!

2. The Strategy Phase

Ask the Holy Spirit to give you keys for further progress. What should I/we do to take them further?

Meet the practical needs that they have.

Do they just need someone who can listen to them? Simply

listening is the best way to really reach people.

Can we find ways to encourage people? Encouragement opens doors.

Plan and complete initiatives (don't wait for them to take the first step).

Create meeting places and connection points. Use people's homes, both yours and others'. Be on the lookout for "third places" in your community, places where people get together when they are not at work or at home.

Impact each other's networks. Invite people from "the team" to come and meet your contacts.

3. The Action Phase

Now you know what you need to do: Write it down, and make a plan for where, and when and how you will do it. Be specific and concrete. Make a plan, week by week.

Get someone else in the church to keep you accountable for seeing through what you have planned to do. This is the most challenging part, but it will be of great help to you when it comes to achieving what you have decided to do.

Get going. Be bold. Be a leader. Lead your friends on those last few steps to Jesus.

Arne G. Skagen

Arne G. Skagen (b. 1957–) has a degree in fire and safety engineering, and for years he has worked with risk- and emergency counselling in Norwegian industry and business. For the last ten years he has been employed in Kristent Nettverk to help different churches inland and abroad to win new people for Jesus. Arne is married, has four daughters, and lives in Bergen, Norway.

Thank God It's Monday! Everyday Evangelism for Everyday People, is Arne's first book.

global giving initiative

As we pursue our mission to help people get their voices and ideas out into the world, we at Unprecedented Press realize that others are concerned with more pressing needs. Finding creativity in every person is important work, but getting food, shelter, and dignity to individuals must come first. That's why Unprecedented Press donates a portion of book revenue to the Everyone Global Giving Initative whose goal is to meet the practical needs of individuals around the world and to share the love of Jesus. To learn more, visit *everyoneglobal.com*

Other titles from

Unprecedented
Press

40 Shocking Facts for 40 Weeks of Pregnancy
Volume 1- *Disturbing Details about Childbearing
& Birth* By Joshua Best

40 Shocking Facts for 40 Weeks of Pregnanc
Volume 2 (*Terrifying Truths about Babies &
Breastfeeding*) By Joshua Best

She Can Laugh - *A Guide to Living Spiritually,
Emotionally & Physically Healthy*
By Melissa Lea Hughes

Once Upon A Year - *Experience a year in
the life of Finn* By Joanna Lenau

Y - Christian Millennial Manifesto
*Addressing Our Strengths and Weaknesses to Advance
the Kingdom of God* By Joshua Best

Y, The Workbook - *A Companion*
By Joshua Best

Crumbs - *100 Everyday Stories about 100 Peopl*
By Rose White